Distant Secrets

An *Autobiography* by
Richard L. Cole

MINDSTIR MEDIA

Published by Mindstir Media, LLC
45 Lafayette Rd | Suite 181| North Hampton, NH 03862 | USA
1.800.767.0531 | www.mindstirmedia.com

Printed in the United States of America
ISBN: 979-8-9862953-0-5 (Paperback)
ISBN: 979-8-9862953-1-2 (Hardback)

CONTENTS

Preface

"I'm not a well-known politician, an influential investment banker, or a sports legend. I'm not even a movie star who thinks he has all the answers to the world's problems. I'm just a normal person. My family and friends would probably say "abnormal," but I'm sticking with normal since I'm the one writing.

Being in my seventies, I find myself reflecting on my life much more than when I was younger. My memories play back like so many highlight scenes from old favorite movies. Each scene pops up accompanied by mental comments such as "Oh, I had forgotten about that" or "I can't believe I was that stupid." Sometimes I get a "Way to go, Richard, you were the man!" and there are always a few "I wonder what would have happened if...?" thoughts.

Those old memory highlights came in handy when my high school class of 1962 was preparing for one of our reunions. The organizers gave us a homework assignment to provide some information about our lives since high school that could be posted on the reunion website.

I started writing, but I just couldn't get the ideas flowing, thankfully, it turned out to be easier than I first thought. All I had to do was relax and let the old memories play back in my head while I took notes.

As I wrote about myself, I made it a point to be very honest, although I'm not sure that's expected when you're trying to look good for your old school friends.

I included representative highlights of the good and the not-so-good, and it wasn't long before it was finished. There it was, my entire life's story reduced down to a page and a half. It was more than a little depressing. My entire life only filled a page and a half.

That little punch to my ego felt better after I thought about all the interesting and unusual things that didn't make the final cut for that short article. I realized there was more than a page and a half to my life.

That one act of writing down a summary of my life led me to an unexpected and pleasing realization. While I have not conquered the world like every high school kid thinks they will, and I don't believe anyone will be making a movie about my "incredible" life, I have had a good, full life punctuated with many interesting and unusual experiences.

That realization, and having friends telling me I should write a book, got me thinking about it. I had never written a book, and since I had suffered a condition that made it difficult to read, I found the idea both challenging and appealing. Then it started; a little but highly annoying voice in my head joined in to pester me. "Write a book, write a book, write a book."

That is why I wrote this book. The next question is, why should you read it? Well, I think you will find it interesting, entertaining and worth the price, but I can't guarantee that. However, I can guarantee that every story and every event I describe in this book is presented just the way it happened. I promised myself I would keep it factual.

Oh, I should also let you know I have not used the real names of many people mentioned in this book. But, if they want to tell you it was them, that's fine with me.

I Got Lucky

I was adopted in 1946 at the age of two, given my new, permanent name, Richard Cole, and officially became the son of Frank and Eloise Cole. I always knew I was adopted. Mom and Dad never tried to hide that from me. They told me my father died in the war, and my mother was killed in an automobile accident. Whenever the subject came up, mom would also tell me they could have chosen any baby, but they picked me. She would then add, "other parents had to take what they got." I think I got lucky.

As I grew older, I began to doubt that story about my biological mother and father. It seemed too simple; parents died, you were adopted, end of the story.

From what I remember as a teen, all my friends thought their parents could not possibly be their birth paents. They believed, well fantasized, they had been lost, kidnapped, or switched at birth, and someday soon, their real parents would show up and claim them. Their real parents would be rich and famous, of course.

While those kids had no chance of their fantasy occurring, I felt there was an outside chance, a possibility, it could happen to me. Maybe not the rich and famous part, but I thought it was likely I had close biological family members out there somewhere. But while the mystery of my origins always lurked in the background of my mind, oddly, my curiosity was never strong enough for me to search for answers until I was much older. I think that is another tribute to Mom and Dad. I don't remember ever wishing for other parents.

Frank and Eloise Cole were caring, supportive parents. Dad was born in 1905 and worked as a millwright at the local steel mill. His dad had worked there before him, and one of Dad's brothers also worked there.

Dad was the oldest of four brothers and never finished elementary school. I don't think he attended school much at all. He could not read or write except to sign his name, but no one except Mom and I knew that.

Mom kept the household running, took care of me, and helped out at church and the school's PTA events. My Mom only made it through the tenth grade, but she was smart. Mom and Dad's lack of education was more a sign of the times and the area of town where they lived than anything against them.

I have few meaningful memories of my life before I was about five years old, but after that, I remember a childhood filled with many things a boy like me could want. I had friends my age to play with, trees to climb, a

Mom on the back porch where I grew up.

creek to play in, and a large tract of undeveloped woods behind our house to explore. We never had much money, but it was a good, formative period of my life.

All the years that took me from bicycles to cars seemed to go so slowly. I didn't think I would ever grow up to be one of the big kids. However, time did pass, and I survived that period relatively intact. Even better, Mom and Dad had not returned me to the county adoption agency as a defective item.

I don't want to give the impression that I was a bad kid, because I never got into serious trouble. I even served as an altar boy at church and was active in the Boy Scout program earning my Eagle badge, Scouting's highest rank. But looking back from my perspective as a parent, I know many of my little adventures and occasional lapses of good judgment gave Mom and Dad plenty of anxiety and probably hastened their gray hair. One of those times came soon after I became a teenager with a car.

Although I was working a lot at the local drive-in diner, school was out for the summer, so I had more free time to work on my old 54 Plymouth. I was slowly fixing it up to look better and go faster, of course. While the old Plymouth wasn't a cool car like a '55 or '57 Chevy, it cleaned up nicely. New, larger tires, new wheel covers, touch-up paint here and there, and a good buff and wax job made it look so much better. The addition of glass-pack style mufflers added a low rumble and made the engine sound much stronger than it was.

"Hey, Dad, Wayne and I want to go out to the drag races on Saturday, ok?" "No, Sir, we are just going to watch." "Yes, we'll be careful, thanks, Dad."

Well, that "we are just going to watch" comment sort of ran out of gas after we got there. Wayne, looking at the cars in the group I would race against, kept saying, "You can beat that one." "Yup, you can beat that one too." So, disguised as my best friend Wayne Smith, the devil made me do it. I paid the fee and entered the race.

I was assigned to a small group of lightly modified street-legal cars with similar power. I had no delusions that this group contained real race cars, and I referred to them, including mine, as poor boys' hotrods. There were four cars in our group that day, and one of them would win a trophy.

Drag racing was something I had never done, and I just couldn't resist it because I would be able to drive as fast as I could and not get a speeding ticket.

My first competitor was a shiny black Mercury, sitting up in the back and looking fast. The countdown lights turned green, and we took off down the track. The Mercury started faster, but I finished faster and won the race!

The next two cars raced each other, and the winner would race me for the trophy. I pulled up to the start line and waited for the other car. The other car did not show up and they announced that the driver had dropped out. I like to think he saw my awesome performance and knew he had no chance to beat me, but he probably had a mechanical problem. At that point, all I had to do was make a solo drive down the quarter-mile track to win the trophy.

I could have taken an easy Sunday drive and circled back to pick up my prize. I still don't know why I felt the need to go as fast as possible. Logic and reason advised me to take the easy drive, but I wanted to go fast. I just had to show off.

When the light turned green, I revved the engine and released the clutch. My car lurched about ten feet and rolled to a stop while emitting the sound of grinding gears. Each attempt to accelerate was met by the sound of crunching metal and very little movement. To put it in non-technical terms, I broke it.

A track official ran over and asked what the problem was. I guessed that the rear differential had broken, but it would still go, sort of. He informed me I had 5 minutes to complete my run without assistance or I would be disqualified. In a sport where nonprofessional street-legal cars of the day could eat up a quarter-mile track in less than twenty seconds, I had forever to get there.

I ever so gently eased out the clutch and pushed the gas a little, and the car slowly rolled forward. I was about a fourth of the way down the track when the announcer, a real comic, whipped the crowd into a frenzy of cheers and laughs. "We will have to hose down the track after this blistering run." "You paid for excitement, folks, and here it is!" "Look at that car go!"

I finally made it across the finish line, and the announcer started shouting over the PA system, "It's a new track record, a new track record, ladies and gentlemen. It's official, that was the slowest elapsed time ever recorded at this track! Let's give him a big hand!"

I knew a lot of the laughing was at me and not for me, but I also knew a lot of the cheering was for the underdog who would not quit. At least that's the way I prefer to remember it. And to all the people in the audience laughing at me, I had just one thought, "I have a winner's trophy; where's yours?"

The winner's high came to an abrupt halt back in the pit area when reality interrupted my party. I was not supposed to be racing and my car was broken at the drag strip. Wayne, sensing that I was in panic mode, came up with a way out. "The car made it down the track, so maybe it can make it home." Then he added, "Even if we don't make it back, we're broke down on the road and not at the drag strip." Thank you, Wayne. We headed out very, very, slowly. We only made it a few miles.

"Oh, hi Dad, well, the car broke down, and we need to get it towed back home. What's wrong? I think the rear end is busted. It started grinding, and now it won't go at all. No, Sir, we are not at the race track; we are a few miles from there. What? Was I racing? Well, uh, uh, I um, yes Sir, but just a little. Yes Sir, Yes Sir, but I won a trophy. I'm going to win what when I get home? Yes Sir, bye." I just could not lie to my parents. I looked at Wayne; he was just slowly shaking his head. He knew our racing days were over.

My racing days really were over, but that was actually my choice. I had a short one-race career and went out a winner, but I could have gotten into it in a bigger way if I had really wanted to. My Dad was always supportive of things I wanted to do, and I know he and the mechanic next door would have joined in to put a little weekend racing team together. But there was a new girl at school, and she was getting more of my attention than my old car.

She had transferred to my school early in our junior year. Her name was Sandra Brooks, she was really nice, and we seemed to get along well. I helped her get acclimated to her new school and introduced her to my friends. Soon most of my weekends were spent going on dates with her, and my backyard hotrod was demoted to basic transportation.

By the time the Junior Prom came around, Sandra Brooks and I were in a steady relationship which made deciding who to go with a lot easier. We were all dressed up in our formal attire and waiting for the stretch limousine to pick us up, just kidding. Our limo that night was my parent's three-year-old base model, four-door Chevy Biscayne, but it was substantially more refined than my old hotrod Plymouth.

The dance was held in the school's gym, and we were having a great time dancing, joking around, and talking about where we would go after the dance when I noticed a teacher cutting across the gym floor straight toward me. "What did I do this time?" was my first thought. As I was escorted out of the gym toward the main office, everyone else also wondered what I had done.

The teacher told me I had a call from my mom and I could take the call there in the office. Mom, crying and scared, told me Dad was being placed into an ambulance and was headed to the hospital. He had collapsed, and the paramedics thought it was a stroke. I told the teacher what had happened, called Sandra's parents to tell them where we would be, and headed downtown to the hospital.

I do not remember many of the details of that night. It all seems somewhat blurred. When we arrived at the hospital, Mom was still scared, but Dad was doing better and resting. He was only 56 years old and had suffered a stroke. A hard life as a steelworker, cigarettes, and southern cooking had taken a toll. Fortunately, it was not a severe stroke, and he would make a slow but steady recovery. His textbook symptoms of partial paralysis on his left side and difficulty with speech would dissipate over the next few months.

By the time Dad's stroke symptoms were mostly gone, a friend asked him to join a bowling league, and his doctor told him that would be great exercise. So, Dad joined the league, and I joined along with him. About three months into the league season, all of Dad's symptoms were gone, and he had become a decent bowler. My bowling scores were also improving. I threw the ball fast and straight. It wasn't pretty, but it was somewhat effective. I was averaging a score in the 170s per game. Not too bad for a beginner.

In early 1962, my senior year in high school, the bowling league season was down to its last few months. That night's games were over, and I was still sitting at our lane while Dad was over at a table looking at the next season's schedule. A man walked over to me and introduced himself. I didn't know him but had seen him at the bowling alley a few times. I remember him because he was a perfect candidate to play a Mafia boss in a movie.

Bob was probably in his mid-forties, stocky but not fat. He was a nice-looking man with dark curly hair and a great smile. He asked me how long I had been bowling, and I told him I had just started that season. He asked what my average score was. I told him, and he said something like, "not too bad."

I mentioned I was there with my dad, who took up bowling as his post-stroke exercise program. Bob said he would like to meet my dad, so I introduced him.

After the usual and customary pleasantries were out of the way, Bob explained that he had been watching me bowl for a few weeks and thought I had the potential to be a much better bowler with the right training, and he would like to help. At that point, Dad and I were both wondering why he wanted to help me and where that conversation was going.

Bob was polite and polished and assured Dad that he would not mind spending a little time with me each week since we were all there anyway.

Then he asked my dad's permission to give me a few bowling pointers right then, a nice touch.

We grabbed a score sheet and a vacant lane and started a game. It only took a few frames of bowling to realize that Bob was pretty good. His approach and ball delivery were smooth and precise, and although I was bowling well, he was staying a little ahead of me in the score.

Halfway through the game, as Bob got ready to shoot again, he paused, turned, and told me I would never bowl better unless I changed my bowling style. I felt a little defensive about his blunt statement, but since he looked like a Mafia boss and was paying for our game, I didn't argue. He turned, made his approach, and released the ball. It glided straight down the right side of the lane, and then made a gentle left curve to meet the first two pins just where it should. The pins responded with a chaotic dance as they scattered. He had made a strike, then another and another and another. I had bowled well but Bob was far ahead of me. I decided I wanted to bowl like Bob.

He probably sensed I was appropriately impressed and ready to listen. He started my first lesson by repeating his earlier comment that I would never get any better without making changes. Everything from my approach to my ball release would have to change.

When he asked if I was ready to start, I did not hesitate to answer yes. Bob then helped me select another ball from the rack and explained it would be a better fit for the way he wanted me to hold and deliver the ball. He then demonstrated how he wanted me to change my approach and ball release, and we started another game.

My score plummeted. It felt awkward throwing the ball the way he was showing me. "Give it a little time and a lot of practice; it will get easier," he said. He told me he was there each week at that time, bowling with friends, and he would check my progress the next week. The class was over.

Within a few weeks, my game was getting back to normal, and Bob said it was time for me to have my own bowling ball. A new ball could have the finger holes drilled to fit my hand and the way he wanted me to grip the ball.

We went over to the sales counter, where I quickly discovered that shiny, new bowling balls were very expensive. But with a little negotiating by Bob, I had a better deal. The man at the sales counter went into the back and returned with an old, used, solid black house ball. He would only charge me to plug up the old holes and drill new ones. With the finances settled, Bob sat with me and helped with the fitting process. It seemed like a lot of fuss about three holes in a bowling ball, but the person marking the layout on the ball was agreeing with Bob.

A week later, I had my very own custom-fitted, ugly, used bowling ball. With my new, old ball, my average score dropped again. But, as the weeks went by, my muscles gained the strength and muscle memory needed to hold and control the ball properly. Everything was beginning to feel comfortable again, and my scores were back to where they had been a few months before. It felt like I had gone through a lot of trouble just to be as good as I used to be.

Although I was excited about learning how to bowl like Bob, I was more excited about the coming summer, turning 18, and graduating from high school.

Certified Adults

It seemed the day would never come, but I was 18 and a high school graduate. Both Sandra and I felt so grown as we thought about college and dreamt about careers. Sandra had chosen to pursue a liberal arts degree at West Georgia College, about 60 miles southwest of Atlanta. That was a long drive in those days before expressways. Sandra's parents had applied a little pressure on her to attend a school that would not be conveniently close to where I would be. Her choice was to go there or pay for it herself.

We knew what her parents were doing. They really liked me, but they thought Sandra and I were getting too serious and were just putting a little water on the fire. We were not happy with their decision, but they could have sent her to another state. At least we would get together every three or four weeks, which didn't seem too bad.

I decided to go to the Southern Technical Institute, a local technical school specializing in engineering. Many of its students used it as a transition into Georgia Tech. I chose to study electrical engineering, which was not a big surprise to anyone.

Unlike Sandra, the only pressure I received to attend Southern Tech was financial. Since Dad was on a disability pension, my parents could not help with college costs, and I certainly did not qualify for academic scholarships. Fortunately, the tuition wasn't too high, and I could live at home while attending classes; if I continued working part-time jobs, I could cover the cost of school.

We had our plans set for the fall, and we had the summer ahead of us.

Being out of school for the summer allowed me to work full-time. That let me earn enough money for my basic needs, fall tuition, dates with Sandra, upkeep, and gas money for my old car. I would even have enough left over for my new favorite hobby, bowling, a lot of bowling.

Then, so quickly, summer was gone, and we were college students, certified adults as we saw it. Settling into our new college life routines made high school seem so far behind us and so juvenile.

Sandra's routine changed much more than mine since she was living on campus at her school. My routine didn't change that much. I'd go to school, go to work, maintain my car, bowl with my dad in the 1962-63 league season, and go to bowling practice with Bob every week or so.

Sandra and I did talk on the phone every few days, and we got together about once a month. Sometimes she would come back home, and sometimes I would drive down to her school and make the long, boring, late-night drive back home. I still remember one of those return trips because it turned out to be much more interesting than the others.

I think it was in January; I do remember it was very cold and very late. My old hotrod and I were about 20 miles into the return trip to Atlanta, and I was speeding, a little, maybe more than a little. I was in a hurry to get home because it was very late, but more so because I was freezing.

A few days before that trip my car's heater started leaking water under the dash. I didn't have the money to replace the heater, so I clamped off the water lines, pulled the heater unit out, and dropped it off to be repaired.

That solved the water leaking problem but left the car without a heater and with a large hole under the dash where the cold air could rush in.

That part of the trip was on a dark, two-lane road in the middle of nowhere, and no other cars were in sight. I was cold but happy I was making good time until I was startled by the blast of a siren and flashing lights right on my back bumper. A sheriff's deputy had come up behind me without lights. I slowed down and pulled over.

The officer approached somewhat cautiously and close to the side of the car. I rolled down my window, and he moved up closer, one hand on his holster and the other holding his flashlight. As he pointed the flashlight inside, I was waiting to hear the familiar "Do you know how fast you were going?", but instead, I heard "Keep those hands on the wheel," followed immediately by "What's going on in your lap buddy?". That strange question caught me so off guard that a sense of panic took over, and I froze, afraid to look down.

When I did look, I realized it was a somewhat unusual sight. I was wrapped up like a tamale in an old blanket from just under my arms to just below my knees, with the excess blanket in a big pile on my lap. I'm sure the deputy's brain was struggling to process what he saw.

I explained that the car's heater was broken and the cold air was blowing into the car, so I wrapped up in the blanket to keep warm. He politely but firmly invited me to step out of the car and unwrap, "very slowly, buddy." Then, after assuring him that I was not armed and was fully clothed, he asked me to pull out my license and open my trunk. I think the police have an inborn curiosity about car trunk contents. He took one quick look and said I could close it.

He took my driver's license and walked back to the patrol car. I heard just a few words back and forth from his car radio, then he briskly walked back up to me and told me to wait there until he got back. He kept my license as security, rushed back to his car, turned on the siren and flashing lights, and sped off into the night. Time slowed to a crawl as I waited for him to return, and I began to wonder if he really would return.

After about 30 minutes, a very long and very cold 30 minutes, the officer came back, made a U-turn, and pulled in behind me again. This time he approached without his hand on his gun. He thanked me for waiting, like I had a real choice, and handed back my license. "We caught the guy we were looking for a few miles from here," he informed me.

It seemed they had been trying to catch a local moonshine whisky runner for several months, and that night they caught him.

Being in a good mood, the officer did not write me a speeding ticket, and he even gave me some free advice. "Next time you come through here, how about going a little slower; and get that heater fixed before you freeze your butt off." I think that last part was an attempt at humor. "Yes sir, yes sir, thank you," I replied, and watched him drive off into the darkness again.

I remember thinking how curious that event was. I had assumed moonshine stills and liquor hauling hotrods had died out back in the 1950s. I learned a few years later just how wrong I was.

Other than that little moonshine incident, my life's new routines had become my new normal. Part-time jobs, school, homework, and bowling kept me pretty busy most of the time. But, on one rare Saturday when I didn't have to work, and it wasn't a date with Sandra day, I got a phone call from Harry just after lunch. Harry, a friend from high school, asked if I wanted to go downtown that evening to a live televised dance show. It was Atlanta's version of American Bandstand, and tickets were really hot items, almost impossible to get, and Harry had one just for me.

"Sure, I want to go, but I don't have anyone to dance with." was my quick reply. Then Harry read me the fine print of his generous offer, "My girlfriend's sister is in town. She really likes to dance and needs a partner." It seemed the cost of admission had just gone way up.

I never thought of myself as a great dancer, even though I won a dance contest at one of the school dances. So, I would say I was a decent dancer with a distinct style.

I had a Saturday evening free, I just got invited to the hottest show in town for teens, and I had just agreed to dance with Harry's girlfriend's sister.

As the time for Harry and the girls to pick me up drew closer, two things started bothering me.

One, I felt like I was doing something wrong; like it wasn't right to go to a dance with someone other than Sandra. I knew I shouldn't have felt that way because I wasn't "going out" with someone; I was just going to a cool dance with some friends. I tried to make the guilt disappear by reminding myself that Sandra was going to events and places with guys at her school. I knew that because she would tell me about each one of her casual "non-dates." So, I decided it would be better if I called Sandra after the dance and told her about it.

With that little guilt trip out of the way, my mind was free to imagine a far bigger problem, Harry's girlfriend's sister. I had just committed to a televised dance event with someone's girlfriend's sister. A person who, it appeared, couldn't get a date to the hottest show in town. And, since Harry had called me on the day of the dance, I had to assume that Harry and his girlfriend were getting desperate, and I was at least the third or fourth attempt to get that girl a partner. Maybe I was the only one who did not know Harry's girlfriend's sister.

Images of Frankenstein in a wig were popping into my mind like those Halloween funhouse ghouls that jump out around every corner. I was thinking about backing out, I'd tell them I was sick, and I actually was starting to feel a little queasy by the time they arrived.

"Oh, what have I done?" was the question I kept repeating as I went out the front door. I walked toward the car like a brave man going to the gallows for his execution, holding his head high and praying the rope would break and he would survive.

"Hi there, I'm Vicky, and you must be Richard." For what seemed like ten minutes, I tried to process what I was seeing. "Richard? Yes, that's me." I struggled for something less idiotic to say, and I'm sure I was just staring at her.

Vicky was no ghoul and certainly not related to Frankenstein. She was a gorgeous redhead and so easy to look at, which I had been doing way too long. I finally managed to acknowledge the others in the car, climbed in, and off we went.

The day was looking up. Harry's girlfriend's sister was beautiful, fun to be with, and, as it turned out, a very good dancer.

When we walked into the studio, and I saw those large TV cameras on stands, I finally realized this non-date would be on a live television show. My guilty feeling returned, and I quickly decided it would be best not to be right in front of a camera. "There is more room to dance over here on the side," I told them. It's a long way from the cameras, is what I was thinking.

The show played all the latest, easy-to-dance to songs, and everyone there enjoyed being on a television show. Vicky and I quickly learned how to dance together, and I soon felt relaxed in the safety of the back corner of the dance floor.

The time flew by, and it seemed like we had just gotten there when the show was down to the last song and the dance contest that wrapped up the event.

As the contest song neared its end, I caught a glimpse of some large object moving on my left side. Well, surprise, one of those large cameras had wheels, and it, accompanied by the MC, was rolling straight toward the contest winners for their big moment in the spotlight.

"Congratulations! You are our winners! And what is your name?" I was stuck in the middle between panic and pride. Finally, I managed to get my name correct without a single stammer. "And who is your lovely date?" At that point, I felt like the deer in the headlights. It was suddenly official; I was with a date, a lovely date.

The MC quickly turned from me and began a nice, long conversation with the not-so-camera shy and very lovely Vicky. All I heard was "blah, blah, blah" in slow motion. The MC's final comment, however, was clear enough. "Again, a big round of applause for this lovely couple." Lovely couple? Now Vicky, my date, and I were the happy, lovely couple in a close-up shot on primetime television. "It's ok. Sandra never watches this stupid show anyway." That was the calming thought I kept repeating to myself as we drove over to the Varsity drive-in for chili dogs. After eating they dropped me off at my house, and I never saw Vicky again.

By the time I walked into the house, Mom had taken three phone calls for me. One was from a girl who lived around the corner. She saw me on the show and congratulated me on winning the dance contest. The other two calls were from guy friends wanting to know who the "hot chick" was.

A little later, I received another call. It was Sandra. She had not seen the show, but she had heard from three of her so-called friends wanting to be sure she knew about the "lovely couple" who won the TV show's dance contest. Evidently, Miss Vicky, the love goddess, and I were quite the story burning up the phone lines that night.

I won't bore you with the details of that long, personal, and mostly one-sided conversation, but I'll just say Sandra was not a happy camper. I was having a hard time understanding why she was so upset. I had simply gone to a dance with some friends as a dance partner. I thought it was a little jealousy on her part, like I felt hearing about her non-date dates. But her reaction was far too dramatic for just that. About halfway into our little discussion, I finally caught on. She had been blindsided by the news when multiple friends called to tell her all about it. She was caught off guard, embarrassed, and hurt.

Sandra and I had several very long, candid talks over the next few weeks, and we both came to the same conclusion, we were miserable being separated. The subject of marriage started popping up in our conversations.

There was no big-down-on-one-knee surprise with an engagement ring. Instead, we had slowly, over a few months, mutually decided that we wanted to get married, so we started discussing how we could make our new plans a reality.

What if I had not won that televised dance contest with Miss Vicky Hot Body? I'm pretty sure Sandra and I would not have been contemplating marriage at that time, and I also believe one of us would soon have met someone else, and our bond would have dissolved.

One can always look back at a point in time and speculate about "what if." But, "what ifs" don't exist, only what was. We were just two kids in love contemplating a major change in our relationship.

My relationship with Bob, the bowler, was also about to take a major turn. Bob had been coaching me all during that league season and I had become the bowler Bob thought I could be. By the season's end, I had the highest score for a three-game set in the league, and I also captured the league champion title. I received a nice trophy and a cool "League Champion" patch to put on my bowling shirt.

League Champion 1962-1963

The attention and the huge confidence boost I received were fantastic, but knowing my dad was very proud of me was the best part. And, unlike my drag racing trophy, Dad suggested I put the bowling trophy up on the mantle.

Bob was also excited about my progress and asked if I would join him as his partner at some small, private bowling tournaments he attends every month. Bob explained that the games would be for money, but he would put up the money and give me a share of any winnings. I thought about it. We would go bowling for money; Bob would put up the money, and if we won, I would get a share of the cash. Well, yes, Bod had a partner.

Bob and I made a good team. We never won a lot of money, but we did win. I don't think any of the bowlers made a lot of money over time, but it sure was exciting. Most of the games I attended were private events held after the bowling alleys were closed to the public.

The hefty entry fees for those mini-tournaments would be collected, a payment for the bowling alley would be removed, and the first, second, and third place winners would get their share of the remaining prize money.

Those games moved quickly, and the side bets between bowlers moved even quicker.

With Bob's help, my game continued to improve, and Bob would occasionally talk with me about becoming a professional bowler. I was almost good enough to do well as a pro, and Bob believed I would continue to improve if I kept at it. I had no intentions of quitting; the competition was exciting and winning felt really good.

The regular league bowling season ended on a real high note for me. I was enjoying my new relationship with Bob, and I knew I needed to decide soon about trying to succeed as a pro bowler. But since Sandra and I were about to finish our first year of college, I also knew I had more important decisions to deal with.

A Leaf
in the Wind

As soon as school was out for the summer, Sandra and I told our parents we wanted to marry. To our total surprise, there wasn't any resistance to our plans. However, Sandra's parents strongly suggested we wait until the following spring. We agreed and set the date as May 10, 1964. We had a lot to do and learn before then.

Sandra's dad was educated and had a law practice specializing in criminal law. He wasn't one of those highly paid corporate attorneys, but they managed a good middle-class lifestyle. My family was a few steps lower on the socio-economic ladder, but I never felt the least bit looked down upon. They were good people.

Sandra and I had spent the summer of '62 preparing for college, but the summer of '63 was spent wrestling with more complex issues. The first was what to do about college. We looked at the possibility of attending a local college and living in one of the dorms for married students. That sounded like a perfect plan- continue school and live together. It was a nice dream, but that dream required far more money than we had because, at that time, all we had was what I made at the hamburger stand. So, higher education got crossed off our "to-do" list.

It was obvious we needed more money. I wasn't long out of high school, and decent jobs were hard to find for everyone, especially kids. But I did manage to get a full-time job working in the produce department of a grocery store, and Sandra found a clerical position at an insurance company. We had found real, full-time jobs and began planning for the wedding and looking for a place to live.

We chose an apartment not far from our parents' homes. It wasn't the best neighborhood, but the rent was lower than other nearby places. It would be our first place, which somehow made the small, old apartment look better. As the big day approached, we scavenged some furniture and gladly received some leftover furniture from a few relatives.

Sandra's aunt's early cash wedding gift let us buy enough groceries and staples to get started, but we were shocked that all that money just bought the basic necessities. We quickly learned that running a household was not as cheap or easy as our parents made it look.

As the big wedding day approached, Sandra and I, with the help of our parents, finalized all the details for the wedding. We decided to have the service in the Catholic Church my parents and I attended. It was a small wedding but had everything it was supposed to have. Sandra was in a wedding dress, and I wore a rented tux. We had organ music, a best man, bridesmaids, and Sandra's youngest sister was the flower girl. The reception was held in the church basement, and unbelievably, the whole wedding event went just as planned.

As soon as the reception was over, we left for our honeymoon getaway. Sandra's dad had arranged for us to stay at a small, isolated lake cabin in north Georgia, only 80 miles north of Atlanta. We had the place for as long as we wanted, compliments from a client of Sandra's dad. It would have been nice to stay there a few weeks, but we only had four days before we needed to return to the real jobs we had found.

Things were really looking good. Sandra and I had jobs. We had just bought a small new car, rented an apartment, got married, and were on our way to a remote cabin in the mountains. On the way, we stopped and bought enough groceries to last a few so we wouldn't have to go back out for a while.

When we arrived at the cabin, we discovered the gallon of milk had leaked almost a quart of its contents into the back floorboard carpet. While Sandra set up the kitchen, I wiped up the milk the best I could without carpet shampoo and a wet vac. There was no way I would spend the first night of our honeymoon looking for a carwash.

It was still light outside when we finished eating, so we decided to take a walk down by the lake to let the meal and our nerves settle a bit.

By that time in my life, I had acquired a fondness for snakes. I loved to find and catch them. Of course, I would never hurt one; just catch it, observe it and then release the snake. It was an unusual but fun hobby.

A snake stick is basically a broom handle with a curved metal rod on the end, used to control a snake during capture. I never went anywhere without my snake stick. Sandra had never been snake hunting and we had an hour or two to walk around and relax. What better time to take her snake hunting?

Sandra and I were a great example of opposites attract. While I was somewhat of an adventure seeker, Sandra was a much calmer, stay-at-home, and make-a-dress type of person. But, to her credit, she was willing to try new and different things, including snake hunting on her honeymoon.

It was a pleasant, although hot, evening, and we were enjoying the walk along the lakeshore, although I had not spotted a single snake. I'm sure that was just fine with Sandra. But just as we got back to the path up to the cabin, I saw small ripples in the dark water only about a foot off the shoreline. It was a snake gliding slowly along. The light was dim, and I couldn't see it very well, but it appeared to be a Brown Water Snake.

That day was getting better and better. It was a large, non-poisonous snake, and it was time to show off for my new bride. The snake sensed our presence and froze in place, head slightly above the waterline. I eased closer to the water's edge and gently slid the curved metal rod on the end of my stick under the snake about a foot behind its protruding head. I was in a perfect position to lift it and grab it just behind its head, but the snake decided that remaining motionless was not in its best interest. It started to swim away. I jerked up on the stick, pulled the snake's front out of the water, and made a sensational grab, catching the snake about two feet behind its head.

When I stood up with my prize, I noticed it was a far bigger prize than I had thought. I looked at it, and it looked at me, and Sandra squealed. I quickly dropped the stick and grabbed the snake just behind its head with my free hand preventing it from turning to bite me.

That thing was almost five feet long and bigger around than my forearm. It was a proud moment as I stood there posing with that snake. It was, however, a very brief proud moment.

The snake flipped the remaining three feet of its strong, heavy body over my arm and, with a quick twist, jerked its head out of my very firm grip. Before I finished saying, "Hey baby look what I caught," it had my puny little forearm in its very large mouth.

The snake started working its jaws, much like enjoying a fine steak. Its jaw slowly flexed side to side as it pulled more of my forearm into its mouth. It was making sure every tooth was firmly embedded into its victim.

I tried to appear calm and even managed a somewhat convincing "It's ok, I'm all right" to calm my horrified wife.

That was not the first time I had been on the wrong end of a mad animal, so I knew what to do. After a brief pause to shift out of panic mode and kneel down, I put my arm on the ground and released my grip on the snake's body. After a moment, the snake responded in kind. It released its jaws and backed off my arm.

As I knelt there with blood trickling from the numerous small holes on both sides of my arm, the snake slid slowly back into the dark water and disappeared.

All the way back up the hill to the cabin, I made excuses about how that snake was able to get loose and eat my arm. Sandra didn't say too much.

The remaining days flew by without incident. Of course, we did not go snake hunting again, but we spent time walking along the shoreline, taking the canoe out onto the lake, and dreaming about the future.

Together we had started a new life. We were on our own; married, and on our own. It was a wonderful dreamlike feeling.

That wonderful feeling ended abruptly on the morning we were leaving the cozy mountain cabin. As soon as we opened the car doors, we were hit with an unbelievably horrible, gagging stench. The remnants of the milk that had spilled in the back of the car had been in the closed hot car since we parked it days earlier.

It would take another chapter in this book to fully describe just how bad that smell was. But after spending another half an hour holding our breath and working with soapy water and rags, it was much better. A short test drive confirmed that as long as the car was moving with the windows down, the fresh air flowing in made the situation at least tolerable.

We headed back to Atlanta, and everything went well for about ten miles. Then we saw the large sign that read, "Road construction next 5 miles, be prepared to stop". The road was being paved, and for most of the five miles, we were crawling past or stopped next to fresh, steaming hot asphalt pavement.

It was a very hot, humid day with no breeze. We could not close the windows because of the rancid milk smell, and the acrid fumes and hot steam from the fresh asphalt kept drifting through the open windows to mingle with the resident aroma of the spoiled milk.

Sandra spent that part of the trip with her hand poised on the door handle, ready to open it quickly in case her queasiness got any worse. I fared a little better, but still had to suppress my gagging reflex more than a few times. Those five miles, at five miles per hour, seemed like they would never pass. But, soaked in sweat and probably looking a little green, we finally got through that highway paving hell and made it back to our apartment and our new life together.

When I returned to work, the first thing I was asked was, "Did you have a memorable honeymoon?" A vicious, monster water snake tried to eat me, and we were almost asphyxiated in a car that smelled worse than a bag of roadkill skunks. Memorable? I couldn't forget it if I tried.

After the exciting start, married life quickly settled into a routine shared with many married couples. Get up, go to work, come home, cook, clean, and look for ways to pay the bills. We did have some time to do other things, but our options for fun and entertainment were very limited without extra money. But it didn't matter; we were young, in love, and making it on our own.

A year later, it became obvious there actually were fun things we could do without money. Our daughter Elaine was conceived on my 21st birthday.

Sandra's parents and mine were super excited about becoming grandparents, and Sandra couldn't wait to tell her girlfriends the news.

Me, I was just scared. Excited, yes, but very worried. A baby meant more expenses, and we were barely getting by as it was. As a matter of pride, there was no way either of us would ever ask our parents for help, so we were, by choice, on our own.

To cut expenses, we downgraded from our cheap two-bedroom apartment to a smaller and even cheaper single bedroom. I also got rid of my fairly new car along with its payments and picked up a much older and far cheaper used car. After that, there wasn't anything left to cut.

I understood the obvious, earning more money would help the situation, but I did not understand how to find a better job. I also did not understand why I didn't already have a great job like the people I saw living in nice places and driving nice cars. It would take a few more years before I figured that part out.

The following is a list of the jobs I held up to that point in my life. It does not go into detail for most of them and does not pinpoint exact dates and lengths of employment, but you'll get the idea.

1955, age 11: Coca-Cola sales - For a few years in the '50s, Coca-Cola offered a Coca-Cola stand that looked like a well-made kid's lemonade stand, except it had a nice metal sign over it with the Coca-Cola logo. I signed up to be a neighborhood dealer. Once a week, the Coca-Cola truck would come by and restock my supply of Coke in bottles and pick up any returning empty bottles. I took orders and delivered them around the neighborhood. I even deliver them cold for a little higher price.

1956, age 12: I started cutting grass up and down the street and made more money than selling the cola, but I didn't quit the cola sales job.

1957, age 13: Flying Saucer Burgers - It was the height of the flying saucer craze, and a Flying Saucer Burgers drive-in opened about a half-mile away. I got a part-time job cleaning up the litter in the parking lot. It did not pay much, but I got free burgers and shakes. They were very good.

1958, age 14: Grocery bagger at a small grocery store. I worked there on weekends and learned to bag groceries, stock shelves, and clean up.

1959, age 15: Public swimming pool locker room attendant for the summer.

1959, age 16: Jacob's Drug Store - I stocked shelves, unpacked and checked in deliveries, and helped customers with selections. I recommended the store brands, which earned me a small commission.

1960, age 16: Crompton's Restaurant - I bussed tables and washed dishes.

1961, age 17: Wingo's Drive-In - This was a cool diner-style restaurant with drive-in service in the back. I worked as one of their roller-skating curb service waiters. I was a junior in high school and worked with two good-looking college girls. My male friends thought I had the best job in town.

1961, age 17: I started bowling in organized leagues with my dad.

1962, age 17: I met Bob the bowler and "worked" to improve my game.

1962, age 18: Carrol's Hamburgers - I made burgers, fries, and shakes at this McDonald's clone.

1962, age 18: Fuller Brush Man - Fuller Brush men sold Fuller Brush products door to door. This was an interesting sales job that I was actually very good at, but I just did not enjoy it.

1963, age 19: The Traffax Reported - In the days before fax machines and the internet, I drove around to various city and county police departments to obtain copies of traffic accident reports for auto insurance companies. Sandra's older brother started this service and was entering law school, so I took over his small operation.

1963, age 19: Big Apple Supermarket - Produce clerk. This was a real full-time job and paid more than the hamburger job.

1964, age 19: "XYZ" Aluminum - I worked the night shift at this aluminum manufacturing plant that made framing for storefront windows and doors. I swept the floors and cleaned the machines that polished the aluminum framing.

1964, age 19: I married Sandra, my high school sweetheart. While not technically a job, marriage does require skill, effort, and dedication.

1964, age 20: "XYZ" Aluminum - I transferred to a daytime job at their warehouse facility and packed aluminum frame orders for customers. While there, I was asked to represent the union at a meeting with management to discuss equal pay for equal work issues for workers at the plant and the warehouse. Since I had worked at both, I was chosen to represent the union's side of the argument.

At the meeting with the company VP and his staff, I made several great, unarguable points for boosting the pay of the plant workers. Management must have thought so because a supervisor with a stopwatch and clipboard followed me around the next week while I packed orders. I was terminated a week later for poor job performance. I never saw that coming. My sense of playing social and political games was not well developed. I'm not sure it is much better today.

1964, age 20: "XYZ" Finance Company- I became a "skip tracer" for this low-end, somewhat shady loan company. I would track down people who were not making their loan payments and could not be contacted. They had "skipped out," usually not far.

After being in the field for a month or two, I learned three things. First, I was very good at finding people. Second, I absolutely hated the job. Number three was a little detail they forgot to tell me in the interview. I had replaced another skip tracer who tracked down his man, who blasted him off a two-story apartment porch with a shotgun.

About a week after learning of my predecessor's fate, I found my man, one of the company's most wanted for non-payment. The company had been trying to contact him for months. I searched and followed leads for about a week when I located where he was staying.

The law said I could not knock on a door before 8 a.m., so I arrived early in case he decided to leave early. I parked in front of the house and waited. Finally, at 8:00 a.m., I started walking toward his front door. About halfway there, the man, let's call him Mr. Big, make that Mr. Very Big, jerked the front door open, rushed down the front steps, and came straight at me.

I would have bet any amount of money my reaction to that unfolding event would have included using my very fast legs to leave in the opposite direction. But I just stood there as that huge man taking brisk, long strides, came right up to me. I don't know if I was too stupid to run or frozen in fear, but I just stood there. He grabbed me by the front of my sports jacket with both hands and lifted me straight off the ground. We were looking eye-to-eye because I was then four inches off the ground. Before I could scream, pray or faint, his angry, intense face relaxed. He lowered me back to the ground, released his grip, and started crying and apologizing.

We sat on his porch steps and talked for a while. He promised me he would go to the office and talk to them about the past-due loan payments. I promised myself I would go to the office and resign. I kept my promise. I don't know what Mr. Really Big did.

1965, age 20: Triangle Lanes: I started working part-time at the bowling alley, repairing equipment and cleaning the lanes. My dad was already working there part-time doing the same.

1965, age 21: A man who worked at the bowling alley also installed carpet and linoleum flooring part-time to supplement his income. I joined him in the part-time endeavor for the same reason.

So, there I was, 21 years old, married with a baby on the way, working part-time at a bowling alley, installing floors part-time, and bowling with Bob the bowling gambler. Unfortunately, my employment history to date only contained a wide assortment of short-term, low-skill, low-pay jobs. Those were not the ingredients needed to make a great resume.

My own choices were hindering my ability to advance in life. I was behaving like a leaf in the wind. The winds of circumstance would pick me up, blow me around and drop me. Sometimes I moved forward, and sometimes I was blown backward. Either way, I accepted where the wind dropped me and stayed until the next breeze came along.

My First "Moment"

B ob the bowler and I had been friends for about three years, and we both enjoyed the friendship, competition, and, of course, winning a little extra money here and there.

Some of our games were not at organized events but just with other bowlers looking for a match. The one I remember best started with a call from Bob saying he had two guys looking for a game if I could make it.

Bob had a smooth charm and a big smile and was always up for a match. We all met at the bowling center at 9 p.m., showed our money, and started bowling.

The other guys were very good, but Bob gave me the "look" a few frames into the match. Bob and I had been doing this for a while and knew each other well. The "look" meant he wanted me to hold back if I needed to, and let them win. Now for a competitive person, that is very hard to do, but Bob knew how to play the game and the people.

We all bowled well that first game, but they, no big surprise, beat us by a few points. "Do you fellows want a chance to get your money back," they asked. "Ok, but just one more game," Bob replied, and the real game started.

It seems they had been holding back a little themselves, and they got off to a good strong start. Bob was struggling a little to bowl his best that night, but it didn't matter because I had never bowled better. By the end of six games, we had their money and the bragging rights.

After directing a few "Where did you find him?" comments at Bob, they handed over the last game's wager; we all shook hands, and they left.

I was not always the one who pulled us through a tight game, and that's why we made a good team. We were rarely off our game at the same time.

Bob had trained me well, and I was beginning to consistently bowl at a professional level.

That was the last time I bowled with Bob, and I'm pretty sure Bob didn't do any bowling for quite a while either. He called me a week after the game and asked me to drop by his place to talk. I thought he wanted to talk to me about joining the pro bowling circuit again, but after a few minutes of meaningless, nervous chatter, he told me he would be going away for a while.

I'm not sure I ever knew what Bob did for a living aside from being a bowler. Maybe he said he sold insurance or something; it didn't matter. As it turned out, Bob had a side business making illegal corn whiskey, better known as moonshine and white lightning. Unfortunately, he got caught, and he was headed to prison.

Bob did not fit my image of a moonshiner. He didn't wear coveralls with one shoulder strap hanging down, and he didn't keep a piece of wheat straw dangling from his mouth like an oversized toothpick. He didn't even chew tobacco or live in a shack at the end of a long dirt road in the woods. No, Bob was a nice, normal-looking, educated guy who just happened to operate a moonshine still.

I never saw or heard from Bob again, and never bowled after that either. I really wasn't broken up about the situation. I was sad for Bob, but my time with him was truly a great adventure while it lasted.

I probably could have pursued a career as a professional bowler like Bob and I had often discussed. Or, I could have enjoyed being a top bowler in local league play, but I didn't.

I still think about Bob and bowling occasionally. I wonder about that road not taken and where it would have led me, but that's another "what if" that does not exist. That experience was over, and other things were waiting to fill the void.

I really didn't need another adventure to fill a void in 1965 because I already had enough to handle that year. I certainly wasn't looking for one, but there it was, right in front of me, an article in the local newspaper about a club whose members explored caves. I didn't know there was such a thing. The article intrigued me, and my curiosity demanded I learn more, so I went to one of the group's meetings.

To my surprise, the people there looked pretty normal. They were members of the local chapter of the NSS, National Speleological Society, which is like an Audubon Society for cave explorers. The NSS promotes the discovery, exploration, and conservation of our natural caves.

The members I met were friendly and eager to share information about their love of caves. I learned that there are a lot of natural caves in the northwestern corner of Georgia, only 100 miles from Atlanta, and many of those caves were open to exploring if you knew where to find them. One of the people I met invited me on a day trip to a small cave that was not too difficult to explore, a good cave for beginners.

Unlike Carlsbad Caverns in New Mexico and Mammoth Cave in Kentucky, which are huge, the cave I was taken to was very small, wet, and muddy. It also did not have paved walkways and accent lighting like the tourist attractions. But it was interesting to be underground in a natural, wild cave.

I listened to the cavers, as they called themselves, tell stories about much larger caves that required cavers to rappel down on ropes, ascend back up ropes, and have good endurance. They talked of the large rooms, miles of passages, and the impressive formations of stalactites and stalagmites found in those caves.

The next month I went on another day trip to a larger cave and was even more excited about the new form of adventure I had found. I was hooked and joined the local chapter of the NSS. I had become a caver.

With 1965 winding down and Sandra and I expecting our first child, I finally got a better-paying job. The local steel mill, where my dad had worked and my uncle still did, had an electrician's helper position open. I felt I was qualified since I had a lot of experience with basic electrical repairs and I had studied electrical engineering for a year at a tech school.

Having relatives working there put me at the top of the candidate list and I got the job.

The good news was the pay was far better than I had been earning. The bad news was the work schedule. Steel mills don't shut down; they go 24 hours a day. There were three eight-hour work shifts each day, and all plant operations employees took their turn on each shift. They worked seven days on the 7 a.m. to 3 p.m. shift, got two days off; seven days on the 3 p.m. to 11

My steel mill days

p.m. shift, two days off; then seven days, well nights, on the 11 p.m. to 7 a.m. shift, followed by three days off.

Working hours like that made it difficult to have a normal home life, but the extra pay for the late shifts made it a lot easier to accept.

That job was nothing like being a normal electrician who wires houses. Instead, we maintained the electrical components of large machinery in a sprawling complex of industrial buildings and heavy equipment. That job was hot, dirty, and dangerous, and I found it very exciting. I also got to be the hero who rushed in and got things running again.

Atlantic Steel was a scrap metal processing plant. It did not smelt iron from iron ore. Instead, it reprocessed scrap steel. Steel is just iron that has other elements added to change its characteristics. The mill recycled old cars and other scrap steel into usable steel products

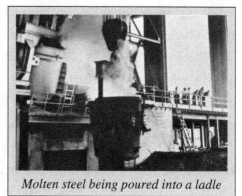

Molten steel being poured into a ladle

like angle iron, rebar, barbed wire, nails, and steel for further processing by other companies.

The scrap was first melted in an electric arc furnace shaped like a gigantic cooking kettle with a domed lid. The furnace's interior, including the underside of the roof, was lined with special fire-resistant bricks to protect the steel walls and roof frame from the intense heat of the melting steel.

The process began by swinging the large roof open and dumping 85 tons of scrap metal into the huge furnace bowl, then repositioning the roof. Three graphite rods, each the size of a small telephone pole and connected to high-power electric lines, would be lowered through holes in the roof until they touched the scrap pile. When that happened, it produced powerful electric arcs, much like a continuous bolt of lightning. The arcs, reaching 3,000 degrees, would melt the steel.

The up and down movement of the large graphite electrodes was controlled by electric motors mounted on top of the furnace roof. Whenever one of those motors malfunctioned, an electrician would need to go out on the furnace roof and fix the problem.

I was lucky, or unlucky, enough to make that type of repair twice during my time at the mill. It was just like repairing or replacing an electric motor or power line anywhere else in the mill except for the intense heat from the molten steel just under the roof.

Every few minutes, I had to get off the roof, splash cooling water on my head and face, and hose down my boots to cool off the soles. I worked as fast as possible because it was unbearably hot on that furnace roof. I also rushed because there was always the possibility that the roof could fail.

The protective bricks lining the underside of the roof's steel frame, like the bricks lining the furnace interior, deteriorate over time due to the extreme conditions inside the furnace. Periodically the furnace would be shut down so the brick interior could be replaced.

One of the keys to lower production costs was running the furnace as long as possible before shutting down and rebuilding the brick interior. Think of it as driving as long as you possibly can on your old car tires before replacing them or having a blowout.

On rare occasions, the brick roof would become too compromised and collapse into the molten steel, producing a thunderous boom and sending an eruption of fire, molten steel, ash, smoke, and searing heat upward. On the roof was the last place you would want to be at that time, because it would be the last place you would ever be.

I don't think I need to mention that this was before OSHA, the Occupational Safety and Health Administration was created. I'm very sure steel mill operations are much safer now.

So maybe there was, or is, something wrong with me, but being out on that roof was a huge adrenalin rush, not very safe, but so very exciting.

Most of the work at the steel mill was not nearly as exciting or dangerous. It was just hard, hot, dirty work.

Sandra, Richard, Mom, Elaine, and Dad. My family in 1968.

I had worked at the mill for about two years and had become good at my job. The bosses and other workers liked me and always asked how my dad was doing. It felt like a family. It felt comfortable there, mentally, if not physically.

Early one afternoon, while I walked across the complex, I passed close to a tour group led by one of the operation managers. He saw me, called my name, and motioned for me to come over to the group. For a moment, I felt I was in trouble for something, but the manager introduced me to the crowd. "I want you to meet Richard Cole. Richard's grandfather worked here, his father just retired from here, and Richard is the third generation of the Cole family to work at Atlantic Steel." He talked a bit about what a great worker I was and how the company was a good place to work. I walked away a little taller and feeling a little pride.

When I got home that afternoon, I told Sandra about the manager showing me off to a tour group and making a big deal about being the third generation of my family to work there. I had not thought of it that way before.

I believe it was two, maybe three, nights later when I woke up abruptly, clear-headed, calm, and mentally alert. It was as if a dense fog had evaporated, and I could see, with stunning clarity, the realities of my life. There they were, so plain and simple, so clear and obvious. I saw myself as I really was, my life as it really was, and the harsh reality that all my dreams and hopes to achieve more in life would never be realized. At that moment, I knew and fully understood that, without major changes in my life, I would spend the rest of my life working at the steel mill like my dad and his dad. I did not sleep the rest of that night.

The best way to describe what I experienced is to call it a spontaneous moment of stunning mental clarity. Although that "moment," that clear, unfiltered view of my reality, felt somewhat spiritual, I don't think it was. But it was a very moving and impactful experience that helped me change the course of my life. I have had other "moments" throughout my life, but only a couple that were so profound as that first one.

Perhaps if I were to practice meditation to achieve higher consciousness, I would have those experiences more often, but my "moments" are somewhat rare, and I'm fine with that. I do, however, give them my full attention when they do occur.

Having a "spontaneous moment of stunning mental clarity" and doing something about it are two different things. To do something about my new insights into the probable course of my life, I actually had to do something. I did not let the fog roll back in and obscure the need to make big changes in my life. I started working on a plan to change my fate, and it felt so good. It felt like I was finally taking control of my life.

In the 1950s, flying saucers and aliens were always in the headlines and capturing our imaginations. By the mid-1960s, computers were the hot topic. "Computers are coming! We will all be out of work because computers will soon be performing all our jobs." But, during those times, news stories and predictions for the future mostly did not happen or even make much sense.

The real news was that businesses were actually moving quickly to automate with computers. Although primitive by today's standards, they still used programs to do their jobs. As a result, computer programming was one of the hot new professions, and it sure caught my attention. Bingo! I had a goal, and I had a plan. Go back to school and learn to be a computer programmer.

I immediately ran into a major problem with my great, new plan. It would be impossible to go to any school while working rotating shifts at the steel mill. Life was handing me a great excuse to give up, to stay where I had landed. But like the ghosts that confronted Ebenezer Scrooge in "A Christmas Carol," my spontaneous moment had put the fear in me. I did not dare let anything stop me from changing my life.

I went to the steel mill's operations manager and told him I needed to change to a position with regular daytime hours because I wanted to go back to school and study computer programming. To my surprise, he did not laugh or tell me to shut up and get back to work; no, he liked the idea. I remember being so surprised at how easy that was.

There was, however, something in it for him. The plant was already planning to add some basic electronic automation to the mill to help control product and materials flow. The equipment the company was reviewing utilized programmable controls and sensors. While not actual computers, the manager liked the idea of having someone around who knew something about the new technology. He made me an offer I could not refuse.

The new position he offered would pay less than my electrician position, and working regular daytime hours would cut back my part-time hours at the local gas station, but I would have a work schedule that would allow me to go back to school at night.

I had a clear goal and a plan to get there. The loss of some income seemed like a small price to pay to get my life on a better track. So, I accepted the new position.

A few months later, I started my new position working in the mill's testing lab as a metallurgical technician. I couldn't even spell it, but that was another very interesting job.

Like cooking a stew and tasting to see what spices are needed, every batch of steel was tested in the lab for its physical properties. Then, depending on the test results, other elements would be added to the mix to give that batch of steel the desired properties.

In the lab, we would test samples of the steel as it was being made and then test the finished products to verify their quality.

By the time I was settled into the new position, it was time to go back to school. There was a good technical school close to where Sandra and I lived, and I enrolled in their new nine-month night class titled "Computer Programming." It does not sound so high-tech today, but back in 1967, computer programming was a new and exciting field, and most people didn't really understand it.

In that course, we learned how computer programs were designed and written to perform specific functions such as processing payroll or updating and printing personnel information.

I was a little intimidated at first because I didn't know anything about the subject I was studying; it was new, sophisticated, and a little mysterious. I found the class material a real challenge, but it quickly became fun and unexpectedly easy. I was very excited by the class and the future it could lead me to.

I was halfway through the computer programming course and already dreaming about life as a programmer when I was summoned to the steel mill office. I walked over there quickly. My excitement grew as I approached the office because I knew I was about to be their first computer programmer.

Well, I did not quite have it right. The steel business had been a little slow, so all new equipment orders were canceled, and the mill was making job cuts to save money. Those cuts included my new lab position.

The good news, and they were very pleased to tell me, was I would be allowed to go back to my former position as an electrician on rotating shifts.

I walked back to the lab very slowly while trying to process that abrupt end to my great plan for improving my life. I felt like crying, but I worked in a steel mill. You don't cry in a steel mill.

I had a wife, a baby, and two choices. I could quit school and go back to my good-paying electrician position or quit my job, stay in school, and face eviction, bankruptcy, and starvation.

My spontaneous moment of stunning mental clarity, and my definitive actions after it, had given me confidence and a determination I didn't have before. I had adopted a new philosophy in my life, and to paraphrase an old saying, "I'll jump off the building and learn to fly on the way down." I did feel confident I could make things work out, so I walked away from the steel mill.

My parents did not share my confidence and didn't understand my decision. Sandra's parents did not understand it either, and I probably don't need to mention what Sandra thought. My decision was described as impulsive, irrational, and immature. I also heard the words stupid and crazy a few times.

I had changed. I had a clear, reasonable goal to accomplish, and I would not let things stop me anymore. I considered my choice necessary, and I was willing to accept a short-term sacrifice to achieve my goal. That type of thinking was new to me. I had confidence, but I was also more than a little scared I might not learn to fly quickly enough.

The Job Interrogation

I must have learned to fly on my way down because I had another job in a few weeks. I became an electrician for an auto parts refurbishing plant. It was a day shift job that would allow me to stay in school, and the pay was comparable to the steel mill. The only downside was the long commute.

I was on a roll and quickly came up with a solution to my two new transportation problems. It was costing me too much for gasoline because of the long cross-town commute in heavy traffic, and my old car was just not up to the long hauls, so I bought a motorcycle. It was a midsize Honda. It was reliable, inexpensive transportation, and fun to drive, except in the rain.

A few days after I got it, we wanted to show it to Sandra's parents. So, after work, Sandra picked up the baby, and we met at her parents' house. Sandra had not been on the motorcycle, but we had bought her a helmet and she brought it with her so we could go for a ride while the grandparents watched the baby. We hopped on the motorcycle and took off to find something for dinner.

It was a great evening for our first ride together, and we soon decided what we wanted to eat. We knew as soon as we caught the aroma from a barbeque shack. Since Sandra's parents' house was so close, we got two quarter chickens with extra barbecue sauce to go.

We put on our helmets and climbed on board. Sandra put her left arm around me and her right arm around the box of chicken, and off we went.

It was getting dark and we were almost to Sandra's parents' house when the narrow road dropped into a little valley in a heavily wooded residential area. Suddenly it was too dark to see.

The motorcycle's headlight had never been adjusted and was pointed straight down in front of the bike. As a result, I could only see the two-foot-wide circle of light on the street in front of the bike. I quickly let off the throttle and started to slow down.

Then I saw it. A solid white line went from the left to the right across my headlight beam. I had just crossed the center line. Before I had time to process that image, two bright lights appeared in front of us as a car coming in the opposite direction dropped into the little valley to join us.

We were left of the centerline looking at two car headlights. I instinctively steered to the right and locked the brakes like a novice rider. The bike went down on its right side and slid down the road. It seemed we slid forever, and all the while, I was waiting for that car to run over us. We finally stopped, and we weren't dead or under a car.

Fortunately, we were not going fast and did not slide far. The motorcycle slid the farthest; I came in second, and Sandra was about seven feet behind me. As I got up to turn off the bike, I asked Sandra if she was alright, and she thought so. I told her to be still and not move until I came back to check her out.

By the time I turned off the motorcycle, the couple from the car had rushed over to see how we were. "Are you guys ok?" the man asked, and as soon as I said, "I think so," his wife, who was walking toward Sandra, let out a loud gasp like she had seen something frightening. I turned and looked back at Sandra and saw a scene straight out of a horror film.

In the harsh glare of the car's headlights, we all saw a swath of meat, bones, and a wide red smear leading to Sandra's motionless body. It took a moment or two, but we all assessed the situation as visually scary but not serious.

Sandra was lying still as I asked her to. The box of barbecue chicken that shielded her from the pavement was now a trail of chicken meat, bones, and red barbeque sauce spread from where she went down right up to where she was lying.

The bike was fine except for some rubber on the right-side handlebar and footrest. Sandra, who rode out the event on me and the barbecue, didn't have a scratch, only some really dirty slacks. I was only bleeding from two places, my right knee and elbow. Both had a bad case of pavement rash.

Back at Sandra's parents' house, I did my best to explain what had happened. That was a somewhat awkward and tense conversation. I had the sense my defense wasn't going well when Sandra stepped in to help. She assured them that she was fine and that I was driving safely and slowly, and that it was the motorcycle dealer's fault for not adjusting the headlights properly.

Sandra also emphasized how my quick reflexes got us back on the right side of the road, albeit with the motorcycle on its side, me on the pavement, and here on our dinner. Her dad was a defense attorney, and apparently, that talent ran in the family.

After a few "We're so glad you both are ok" comments, they noticed I had some holes in my clothes and my skin. Sandra went and got the first aid kit.

I'm not sure about my quick thinking saving us in that minor motor-cycle incident, but my quick thinking did save the day a few weeks later on the way to my computer class. I had gotten home from work, caught a quick dinner, hopped in my car, and headed to class.

It was already dark when I passed an apartment complex on my right, and something caught my eye. Did I see what I thought I did? I wasn't sure, but I stopped, made a U-turn in the street, and drove into the apartment complex. As I drove across the parking lot, I could clearly see the upstairs apartment. There was a dim, flickering reddish-orange glow in a window. It was a fire.

I stopped the car, blew the horn a few times, and ran up the stairs to the apartment with the glowing window. I banged on the door a few times but no answer. I did the same next door, and a lady peeked out a door with a safety chain still in place. I felt like a door-to-door salesman again, having to sell her on the fact that the next-door unit was on fire. Understandably, she didn't seem to believe me at first. I asked if anyone was at home in the burning unit and felt very relieved when she said they were at work.

By that time, there was visible smoke flowing from the outside eaves and curling back into the breezeway. The smell of things burning became noticeable. I told her she needed to get out fast. A young man across the hall opened his door to see what was happening. I guess I was yelling "fire" loud enough to get noticed. I asked him to call the fire department, and then he probably needed to get out of there.

I finished alerting the other residents on that floor and went down-stairs. The young man came down to let me know the fire trucks were on the way. We both then ran down to the next breezeway to warn the other building occupants.

Within a few minutes, the engulfed unit's window shattered, and the smoke and flames were billowing through the opening and out the eaves. By then, it appeared everyone was safely outside just in time to see the fire trucks and police cars pull up to the building. Flashing lights were every-where. My heart was pumping.

I had seen things like this on the news where someone runs in and gets people out to safety just in time. The residents would all come over to thank their rescuer, and a news team puts the camera on him as he tells the viewers that he only did what any normal person would have done. Then the hero is all over the news for a day.

Well, the residents never even looked at me again. I knew they had more important concerns on their minds, but no news team showed up either. Then the policeman, who had been talking to the residents, walked over to me. I thought he would thank me for getting everyone out of the building, but he simply told me to get my car out of their way. I got in my car and went to my computer class.

It's true that many other people would have done what I did if they had seen the fire. I didn't crawl through the flames to rescue children or save someone's pet from certain death, but I still felt good about what I did.

A few months later I finally completed my computer programming course. I really liked that course and actually tied with another student at the top of the class. After that, I did not waste any time searching for a job to put my new skills to use.

One of the companies I secured an interview with was Southern Bell Telephone. It was the Southeast's regional phone service company. I had mailed them my resume with a "why not, stranger things have happened" attitude. A few weeks later, I got the call for an interview. There were many other people there and my interview was short. But I must have done well because they invited me back to take their programming aptitude test.

I joined five or six other people taking the test. I felt a little awkward being there with everyone wearing suits. I wasn't sure what to expect, but the actual test didn't seem that hard, and I was the first one to finish. That worried me because to use another old saying, "If the answers seem too easy, you don't understand the questions."

I was surprised when they called me a few days later, inviting me back for another interview.

I had no idea what to expect for the follow-up interview because I had never been through a hiring process like theirs. However, I suspected they would question me about my work ethic and how I thought I could benefit their company, so I practiced answering questions like those.

I was wrong about their questions, not even close. Three men were sitting across the table from me and the only thing missing from that interrogation scene was the little table lamp shining in my face. They started with many questions about whether I knew or associated with anyone who worked at the company headquarters. I didn't and told them so. I thought the questions they were asking were a little strange.

After a few back-and-forth exchanges, they explained their line of questioning. I had scored higher on their test than anyone before, and they were concerned I had help with the test answers. On the other hand, they seemed pleased with my answers and that I had also scored so well in my tech school computer course. They seemed assured I had not cheated on the test.

The interrogation, however, was not over. "We see on your resume that you did not list your college or degree. Where did you attend?" My response that I never attended college left them a little puzzled. I don't think they knew what to say next.

Someone had made a big mistake. Perhaps someone confused the tech school computer course I listed with a college degree. I should never have received the first interview because they only hired people with a college degree for that position.

They were stuck. I shouldn't have been there, but I had aced their test. With an "excuse us a few moments," they held a brief conference in the hallway and came back in with a good compromise. I could have a job as a programmer if I promised to go to college and work toward a degree.

The Southern Bell headquarters building was located across the street from Georgia State University; the decision was easy. I had a new job and a new career. I was happy, Sandra was happy for me, and we both were happy about the bigger paychecks.

My parents were especially proud and impressed that I worked with computers at the phone company at their headquarters. I think they were just as impressed that I wore a suit to work. It made me feel good because they were pleased. Dad could not read or write and worked at the mill most of his life; now, his son had a fancy job with the phone company. I think my little accomplishment made both Mom and Dad feel they had done a good job raising me. That was never in question.

I had only been at my "fancy" job a few months when I got the call from Mom's neighbor. Dad had died. Mom had been calling from the back porch down to Dad's workshop on the back of the garage. It was time to come up for lunch, but he never answered. He had been dead for a while when Mom finally went down to the workshop and found him. He was just 63.

I got there after the police left and before the ambulance came to take him away. I remember thinking he was probably enjoying tinkering with something on the workbench and collapsed right where he was working. It was quick.

He had enjoyed his last few years working in the shop and bowling in the league. He was happy that I had a fancy job and he had a grandchild.

Nearby neighbors quickly arrived and brought food, friendship, and consolation. Sandra got there shortly after I did, and we helped out with the gathering.

Later that afternoon, several people were still there talking and keeping Mom occupied. She was in her favorite chair with her little Chihuahua lying in her lap when it quietly died.

I have to say this again, sometimes things just happen. Mom had just lost her husband, and then her little companion died in her lap. Maybe it was better to get all the grief over at one time.

Mom took the discovery much better than I would have. She mentioned that the dog was old and maybe all the excitement in the house was too much for it. Mom was a strong woman. We all had a few more tears for her dog, then I placed it nicely in a small box and buried it in the back corner of the yard.

Sandra and I asked Mom to come and live with us, but she really wanted to stay in her own house, so we made a point of driving to her side of town as often as possible, and we had her stay with us a few days every month. I picked up the maintenance on her house, and we made sure she had enough money for groceries, her medicines, and other necessities. Although she was five years older than Dad, she could get around reasonably well and was still driving. She soon adapted to her new life and was doing well.

The following spring, Mom's younger sister's daughter was getting married, and Mom wanted to go down to Miami and visit during the wedding. So, I took a few days of vacation, added them to a weekend, and drove Mom down to Miami.

The wedding and reception were nice and predictable and, like most weddings, not too memorable. However, near the end of the reception, Pam, the bride, asked me to stay later because they would have a real party then. It sounded good to me, so my older cousin Walter took Mom back with my aunt and uncle. After that, the rest of the older crowd left too, and the party started.

By this time in the late sixties, drugs had permeated the young "hip" culture, and marijuana and hallucinogenic drugs were used everywhere. This party was no exception, and there was plenty of beer, liquor, and marijuana to go around. There was a small dance band there, and the music was good, although I'm not sure many of the people there cared or even noticed.

The celebration was not a "tear the house down" wild party; it was just a lot of young friends having fun. I was being cautious not to drink or smoke too much because I needed to drive about 20 miles back to my aunt and uncle's house, and although it was a somewhat straight route, GPS had not been invented, and it was dark.

After a few hours at the party, I told Pam and her new husband congratulations and that I had a really great time at their party. They insisted that I stay a while longer, but I felt tired and needed to head back. They suggested one last toast before I left. Since I wasn't at all intoxicated, I agreed. Her husband went and got us some champagne, and we had a small "happiness and a great future" toast, and I left the party.

On the way back, I was thinking I had eaten too many party snacks because I was feeling a little off. My stomach wasn't cramping or anything; I just felt a little out of it. Just a few more miles down the road, as I approached a roundabout with some palm trees in the middle, things started to get a little weird.

The palm trees in the roundabout started moving, swaying back and forth and growing much taller. I knew I was in trouble when those trees morphed into a large cartoon-like dinosaur in striking colors. I was absolutely petrified. I was going insane.

The inside of the car stretched far out in front of me, but my arms and legs became so long they had no problem reaching the distant pedals and steering wheel. I somehow managed to negotiate the dinosaur-filled roundabout to the other side, where I saw a little line of stores on the right side of the road. The building was swelling up like a balloon and gently swaying back and forth while changing colors. It didn't appear real, but I knew it was despite what I saw. I noticed cars at the end of the building at what seemed like a bar. At least I could still think somewhat clearly and figured that if I parked near but not too close to the bar, my car would not stand out, and no one from the bar would see me in the car.

I was scared, paranoid, and feet very vulnerable. I worried about the police finding me. What would I say or do? Could I even say or do anything? I was going to be in jail for sure.

While my senses, especially my vision, were obviously distorting reality, I could think logically enough to realize I was not going crazy but had been drugged. Strangely enough, that realization gave me some comfort. I wasn't going crazy, just going on a strange LSD "trip." I had smoked marijuana enough to understand its effects but had never taken a hallucinogenic. It was a whole different experience.

I spent the next few hours mostly lying down in the front seat, hoping no one would find me. Occasionally I looked out the window to see if the colorful dinosaurs and dancing building were still out there. Finally, after a little extra waiting to be sure the effects of the drug had dissipated, I managed to get back to the house safely.

Maybe if I had known what was happening and had been in a safe environment, it would have been less frightening and perhaps an interesting experience, but I don't plan to find out. Nevertheless, that unsolicited hallucinogenic trip, as scary and uncomfortable as it was, did give me a perspective and understanding of how hallucinogenic drugs affect people. I'm thankful for that knowledge, but not so much for the experience.

6

A Rattlesnake, Sharks, and Biff

My job as a programmer at the phone company headquarters was going great. I was very good at designing and coding programs, and that was a good feeling. I quickly settled into the corporate scene and was proud that I now had a high-tech office job. The good salary and steady paychecks helped me and Sandra catch up with the bills and even have a little leftover for extra things. For the first time, we both felt we were doing alright.

Although I did like the overall environment at the phone company, I found some of the corporate culture mildly irritating. The phone company management was just like IBM, big banks, and many other large office environments. This was the late 1960s, but corporate dress and personal appearance codes were strict and still stuck in the 1950s.

I didn't have a problem with the suit and tie; I liked wearing them, but my boss and everyone in management did not like to see men's hair touching their ears or shirt collars, and facial hair was strictly taboo. That sounds strange, even laughable now, but those were the rules back then. It seemed to be the college-educated, white shirt, button-down collar, skinny-tie, short hair guys versus everyone not fitting that description. That was the corporate culture of the period.

I looked nothing like the members of the hippie generation, of which there were a lot in downtown Atlanta. No, I dressed just like I should, but I did have thick, healthy, dark hair.

Some years earlier, I got a crew cut just to see what I would look like. One look in the mirror convinced me that short hair was not for me. I kept my hair a medium length, which slightly covered the top of my ears. I had no big sideburns or other facial hair, and the back of my hair barely touched my shirt collar. My hair was always nicely cut and combed, but it was not the short-hair corporate look.

My boss, Biff, never told me to get a haircut, but there were a few subtle hints now and then like, "Is your barber on vacation this month, Richard?" I believe that counted as strike number one against me.

My friends in the caving club had no problem with my hair. Most were office workers like myself, and we all probably used caving as an escape from the hum-drum of normal life and to feed that need for an occasional adrenalin rush.

I had been active in caving for about five years and had been in all of the area's large caves and many smaller, less-known caves. I was even lucky enough to discover new, unexplored passages in a few caves.

But time and the pressures of working and maintaining a family combined to restrict my caving adventures. The caving club meetings were monthly, but actual caving trips only occurred seven or eight times a year, and most were day trips. But still, that was time away from home, and Sandra was not interested in joining me. She wasn't the athletic, adventure-seeking type. Although she did go on one group trip that I was leading, it wasn't her thing. My participation, without her, left her at home with the baby.

My caving days were numbered, but there was excitement in the caving community because some fellow cavers, exploring a new area in a known cave in north Georgia, made a fantastic discovery. A small side passageway ended at a large opening. The cavers' lights would barely illuminate the opposite side, and they could not see anything in the void below.

They had found a huge vertical chamber carved out of limestone by an underground waterfall. Cavers call them pits.

As the story goes, when they came to the end of the passage and looked into the huge hole, they used an old trick to test the pit's depth. Throw a rock in and count the seconds until you hear the sound of the rock hitting the bottom. They threw a small rock into the dark pit, but did not hear it hit the bottom. So, not believing what they heard, or in that case, didn't hear, they tossed in a larger rock, and when they finally heard the sound of the rock hitting bottom, one of them exclaimed, "Fantastic." So that pit became known as Fantastic Pit. It is close to 600 feet deep, about a 55-story fall to the bottom, and it is the deepest freefall cave pit in North America. "Freefall" means the pit is shaped like an inverted cone, so from the point of entry at the top there is nothing to obstruct your descent.

Not long after the pit was discovered, I had the chance to explore Ellison's cave and descend into Fantastic Pit. Rappelling down into the darkness is scary and exciting, but somewhat quick and easy. Making the long ascent back up the rope is a whole different game, and none of us had ever attempted a 600-foot climb. But I was experienced, in great shape, and excited to get started.

The excitement started even before we got to the cave entrance. At the small mountainside clearing where we parked our vehicles, we were putting on our caving clothes and grabbing our gear when someone yelled "snake." I was thinking the day was getting better and better.

I trotted over to the car where the hollering was coming from, and fortunately, I got there just as the others were poised to kill the snake with large sticks and big rocks. I convinced them that it was not going to attack, and it was only rattling to let them know it was there. It was a Timber Rattlesnake, a little over four feet long, and we were in its territory.

The other cavers pointed out that it may be there when we come back out of the cave that night, and they would not be able to see it, which was a problem. To save the snake, I grabbed a sturdy canvas bag that a rope had been in and a sturdy stick with a limb fork at the end. I pinned the rattlesnake down with the stick, grabbed it just behind the head, dropped it into the bag, and put the bag in my car. The rattlesnake would live another day, and nobody would step on it that night. Everybody was happy except the snake. But, being unhappy is much better than being dead. I wasn't even in the cave and was already having fun and excitement.

Fantastic Pit was, well, fantastic. I was the last to descend into that huge dark hole, so I had the advantage of seeing how far away the lights on the bottom were. The caver before me took my camera and tripod down and set them up on the bottom with the camera pointed up. As I started my descent all of us turned off our lights and they opened the camera lens in the total darkness.

I started my descent, stopped a few feet from the top, and set off my strobe flash. I continued the descent in the darkness, stopping three more times on the way down, shooting the flash each time. The resulting picture looked like there were four people on the rope and gave a good perspective of the enormous size of that pit.

Fantastic Pit inside Ellison's Cave in northwest Georgia. Photograph by Willie Hunt and Benjy von Cramon.

Others have since taken far better photographs with much better equipment. The photo shown here really illustrates the size and beauty of Fantastic Pit. If you look closely in the middle of the picture you can see the tiny image of a caver ascending a rope back to the top.

It is a beautiful but also very dangerous pit. At least three people have died, and others have been injured and rescued in the Ellison's Cave complex. I made it home safely.

The Timber Rattlesnake rode home with me in the rope bag on the floor under my seat. When I got home, I had to explain the snake to Sandra. "Well, they were going to kill it, and the only way to save it was to evacuate it to friendly territory." "Where am I going to keep it?" she asked. "Uh, in the bathtub? It's only until I find it a good home."

I chose the bathtub because it had smooth, rounded sides, and I was positive the rattlesnake could not climb out of the tub. Actually, I was only cautiously optimistic, so I kept the bathroom door closed and always entered slowly, just in case. I gave the snake some old towels to hide under and I even gave it a nice meal during its stay with us. I won't go into the meal details.

My first "adopt my snake" call was to the Atlanta Zoo's Herpetology Department, and that was the only call

The Timber Rattlesnake in our bathtub.

I had to make. My snake had three things going for it. First, the Timber Rattlesnake is indigenous to southeastern states. Second, my snake, over four feet long, was large for the species, and third, the zoo didn't have one. The zoo was excited to add it to its collection.

The snake lived out its life in a heated condo with maid service and free food. We all should be so lucky.

I could have used some of that snake's luck back at the phone company.

I still had the motorcycle I used to get back and forth at my last job. I rode it downtown to the phone company on sunny days because I saved on gasoline with the bike, did not have to pay for downtown parking, and it was easier to get through the traffic.

From Biff's point of view, I might as well have come to work wearing a Hell's Angels jacket and sporting a "Born to Raise Hell" tattoo across my forehead. I'm exaggerating a little here, but I did walk into the office with my motorcycle helmet in one hand and a briefcase in the other. Riding my motorcycle to work was probably strike number two for me.

I didn't have a college degree; my hair was too long for Biff's taste; I rode a motorcycle, and I was one of those cave-exploring people. And, while I'm laying out the reasons he didn't like me, let me mention that I was more intelligent than he was. I know how that statement sounds, but the fact was every one of the programmers was more intelligent than he was.

Biff had been a star on a big college football team, and the corporate culture was proud to have him working there. However, I personally thought he may have taken one too many hits to his helmet. I'm not saying I was smarter than Biff, just more intelligent. If I had been smarter, I would have been aware of the interpersonal relationship aspects of our boss and peon arrangement.

Sorry about that little rant. I guess, after all these years, I'm still irritated at that guy. I'm sure Biff was a decent person and was only doing what he thought was best for the company, or maybe for his little ego.

As I promised the company when it hired me, I enrolled in night classes at Georgia State University. I realized that a four-year degree would take forever if I did not take a full load of classes, and even then, the four-year Bachelor of Business Administration degree would take me, well, four years. I was much too impatient to drag something out for six or more years, so I decided to attend full-time at night. It sounded easier than it was. I was working, Sandra was working, she had the baby to care for, and now I was a full-time student. It was hard, but we both wanted me to get a degree to improve my chances of securing even higher-paying jobs.

Since we did have a little extra money at that point, we could occasionally go on short vacations. We still could not afford big trips, but we were content with our short-duration driving trips in the southeast. Our first trip to Panama City was great. We were excited to let our three-year-old daughter see the ocean for the first time, and we were excited to just get away.

Elaine was pointing out to the beach from the back of the motel and babbling something about water. We spent most of that day introducing Elaine to the ocean and enjoying the downtime.

That afternoon we went out onto the large pier to try a little fishing. I actually caught a nice little fish but had no clue what it was. Finally, a guy fishing near us told me what I caught, and we struck up a conversation. My new best friend Rob and I talked and fished while Sandra and Elaine watched the waves, sea birds, and the occasional fish flopping around the pier.

After a while, Sandra came over and said we should probably go back to our motel, clean up, and find dinner. As I gathered my fishing gear, I asked Rob if he would be back out there the next day. He smiled and said he would be back out there later that night when the crowds were gone. He then invited me to join him and his buddy for some shark fishing from the pier. Sharks? Of course, I would be there.

It was well after dark, and the beachgoers and pier tourists had left. The two guys came onto the pier with rods and reels that looked like heavy-duty versions of normal fishing gear. The rods were short and stout, with very large reels holding thick, high-strength fishing lines. The hooks were huge, not even in the same league as freshwater hooks. They were large enough for me to lay my wrist into the curve of the hook. These guys were serious. The cooler they brought contained several large fish cut up into roughly two-pound chunks to use for bait. And the best part was they had a spare rod for me to use.

Since the bait was so heavy, there was no way to cast it like small, lightweight rods and fishing lures, so they showed me how to hang the rod beside the pier, swing it like a pendulum, and then release it on the out-swing. The large bait would travel about fifty feet or so and splash down.

We had just settled in to wait for some shark action when images came to mind of what I had seen people on television do to the sharks they caught. They would kill them. They would shoot them, stab them to death, or cut off their fins so they could not swim. I couldn't be a part of something like that, and I should have thought about that before joining the party.

After a few minutes of planning my excuse for leaving, I ask the question. "What do you do with the sharks you catch?" "We turn them loose." That answer was a great relief.

After about an hour, I watched the process as Rob got a hit on his line. He let the line run a bit, then snapped back on the rod to set the hook, and the fight was on. The shark was pulling out line fast, and Rob was tightening the line brake to slow it down. The shark did not pull out too much line before Rob had stopped its run. "This one is not too big," he said. In about ten minutes, he started reeling the fish in. Before the fish got too close to the pier, Rob let off the line brake and walked quickly down the pier toward the beach. His friend was already down on the beach, and Rob dropped the fishing rod down to him. His buddy reeled in the slackline and moved down the beach away from the pier to prevent the shark from getting the line tangled in the pier pilings. Rob and I quickly joined him on the beach.

It took another ten minutes to pull the shark into the very shallow water at the edge of the beach. The shark was "only" about seven feet long and somewhat slender. Rob's friend pulled the line tight with the shark's head upon the sand, and Rob walked into the water and sat on the shark like he would ride it. His friend handed Rob some large pliers, and Rob carefully removed the hook and dragged the shark back into deeper water. With a few flips of its tail, it disappeared.

Rob's friend said it was too bad that it wasn't big. "Maybe tomorrow night," Rob replied. Tomorrow night? I couldn't wait.

The next night I was the lucky one, and the shark was over seven feet long and much heftier. Rob said it looked to be about three hundred pounds. We all joined to hold it down to remove the hook before releasing it. While I sat behind its head and Rob's buddy held the tail, Rob removed the hook. This was a much larger shark, and fortunately, it was very tired. When we got off of it, the shark did manage to roll over, but that was about all it had left.

We pulled it back into the water and actually walked it around a little in about thigh-deep water until it started getting livelier. Then, we gave it one last shove, and it swam off into deeper water.

Sandra and I were able to get back down there a few more times over the next two years, so I had several more shark-fishing adventures. Unfortunately, we lost track of Rob after our last trip. But, like us, I'm sure he also had real life to deal with. Hopefully, he didn't catch one too big to handle. Either way, thanks for the adventures, Rob.

Back in my real life, things were still going well. It was 1971 and a little past my 27th birthday. I had been a programmer at the phone company for almost three years. That was a new employment longevity record for me.

Sandra and I had moved into a nicer three-bedroom apartment which gave us more room and two bathrooms. That had become necessary with our growing kid and my mom visiting. I had sold the motorcycle and bought a new Dodge Coronet. It was a basic model, but it was new. Things were certainly going well for us.

It was just after lunch on a Friday when I was summoned to the department manager's office. I got a little excited about it as I walked in. I felt a promotion and a nice raise were in my future.

Biff was also there, and the mood appeared much more somber than one would expect for a promotion announcement. The first thing Biff said was I should be more careful about what I keep in my desk drawer. Then he told me I was being terminated for a violation of company policy.

I was totally shocked. What, was I hoarding too many company pens? He went on to say that "marijuana is illegal and is not tolerated at this company." "What are you talking about?" I replied. Biff said he was looking for a good eraser in my desk and found a bag of marijuana. I told them that was totally impossible. "I know what I saw," he fired back. At that moment, I had a slight chuckle of relief because I realized what he had seen.

I asked if I could get the bag and show it to them. You would have thought I had said, "Ok, I'll turn over the illegal drugs and sign a confession.". The big boss said "yes" with enthusiasm.

I brought the baggy back into the office and opened it. I explained that it was not marijuana but Rabbit Tobacco, a harmless aromatic weed that grows all over the place. When I was a kid, my friends and I would roll it up on pieces of paper and smoke it before we were old enough to buy cigarettes.

I told them another programmer, Vince, and I were discussing our youth, and I mentioned Rabbit Tobacco. Vince had never heard of it, so I brought some in to show him. "You can ask Vince. You can even have it tested. It's not marijuana. It's just a harmless weed." I only received stern, blank stares in return.

I wanted to point out that Biff was an idiot since he could not tell the difference between marijuana and Rabbit Tobacco even though there was no resemblance between the two plants. But that would imply I was a little too knowledgeable about the subject. I wanted to ask why Biff was snooping around in my desk drawer in the first place. I also wanted to ask Biff why he assumed I could be stupid enough to leave a bag of marijuana in my top desk drawer. I wanted to ask them why they were doing that to me. I wanted to ask all those questions, but it didn't matter; the fix was in, and I was out. Strike three was Biff's fastball, and I never saw it coming.

To make it more humiliating, they had a security guard escort me to clean out my desk while everyone silently watched. I was shown the door and went home.

Why didn't I see this coming? What did I do wrong? What's wrong with me? What am I going to do now? How can I tell Sandra? What are we going to do for money? I had no answers, just questions. Where are those spontaneous moments of stunning mental clarity when you really need one?

By the time Sandra picked up Elaine at daycare and got home, I was composed and acting normal. I wasn't ready to tell her. I couldn't do it. I needed time to think, to find a way to fix everything. I got through the weekend and pretended to call in sick on Monday. After Sandra left, I started working on a resume looking in the paper for help wanted ads, and calling recruiting firms.

Tuesday was just like Monday, but I confronted my situation midway through the day. There was absolutely no way I would have a new job in a few days. "Oh, hi Sandra. Did I happen to mention that I left the phone company last week, and now I have a great new job?" That wasn't going to happen, and I had to face reality. I told Sandra that night. Although she tried to sound sympathetic and upbeat, I knew I had let her down, and she, like me, was worried.

A Trip to Heaven

Fortunately, the fear and insecurity of unemployment and the mind-numbing routine of looking for a new job did not last long. Just a few days later, I talked with our neighbor across the hall. She mentioned that she was looking for someone with electrical and mechanical experience in a small startup company. I interviewed and got the job. That was quick and easy. The downside was that the pay was much lower than what I had been making. It was, however, a lot more than nothing.

A local entrepreneur had decided that the world needed a machine that would allow you to view microfiche film documents and make copies of what you were viewing all in one machine. Every institution that stores images on microfiche would want one. The idea man had found some investors and hired people with microfiche readers and copying machine design experience. Lucky for me, they also needed a jack of all trades to help set up a shop for making prototypes and, eventually, the production line. The new startup business became my new career.

I learned a lot about image copying devices' optical and mechanical functions, and I listened to the entrepreneurs and the investors haggle about funding, ownership percentages, stock options, and when there would be actual working models. I found those glimpses inside a startup business much more interesting than the day-to-day hunt for parts and equipment to build a working prototype machine. I even bought a little of their stock and ended up selling it at a small profit to another investor looking to buy up additional shares in the young company.

That November, the owner came to me needing help with a business question. The design stage was wrapping up. We had built a few working models pretty much by hand, and now it was decision time. Do we set up to manufacture the units in-house or have another company make them? The owner wanted my input and advice on this crucial decision. I was flattered that I had an important role to play. I got busy contacting and soliciting bids from other companies to build our machines. I also began calculating the cost and time to set up production in-house.

After three weeks of concentrated effort, I had my time and cost estimates for in-house production and the preliminary quotes from two companies interested in producing the new microfiche reader-printers. In my opinion, it wasn't even close; now that the design work was complete, it would be far faster and definitely cheaper to outsource the manufacturing process.

The week before Christmas, everyone except the owner, the engineer, and my neighbor, the secretary, was terminated. They were in talks with one of the manufacturers to take over production- this time I gave myself good marks for situational awareness because that decision didn't blindside me. I didn't, however, think it would happen one week before Christmas.

That Christmas holiday cheer was replaced with anxiety and worry since I was unemployed again, and, oh yeah, surprise, Sandra was pregnant again. Ho, Ho, Ho, Merry Christmas.

That Christmas was hard to get through, but the New Year brought new hope. I quickly found another job, a real job with decent pay. I became a programmer for the Atlanta Public Schools. It entailed the same kind of work I did for the phone company, but in a much more progressive, laid-back, and creative work environment.

I had landed on my feet once again. It was a good job, with no hassles about my hair or lack of a degree, and I loved the work atmosphere. Another positive of this job was that the school system data center was also just a few blocks from Georgia State University. So, with only a short intermission, I was back in college full-time at night.

That May, our son Michael was born. I had heard that the second child delivers faster than the first. In our case, that seemed to be true. Michael was on a fast track to enter the world. As soon as labor started, we contacted the doctor, who said we could come on in and he would be there later. Sandra and I arrived, and she was placed in a holding room to see how labor would progress. Times had changed since Elaine was born, and I was allowed to stay by Sandra's side. That worked well because shortly after arriving, Sandra pushed the button to call the nurse; the nurse said, "Uh-Oh!" and the nurse and I pushed the bed down the hall to the delivery room.

The doctor was paged and replied he was at the hospital and would be right up. He arrived just in time to say congratulations, you have a healthy baby boy. The nurse had already handled the delivery. Actually, she just caught Michael as he entered the world, and I handed the nurse the things she needed during the process. That experience was far better than the old way. We were officially a family of four.

I received a promotion and a nice raise at the school system by the next year. I also started working some overtime each week because the data center had begun a complete rewrite of the school system's outdated accounting system. The extra money was great, but the extra time at work plus going to school full-time and the associated homework did not leave much free time. The upside of all the overtime was saving for a down payment on a house.

We came up with a budget for a house and then started looking. We soon found a new neighborhood we liked in a small city just North of Atlanta. The commute would not be too bad, and the subdivision we liked was new and solidly middle class. Every pre-built house we looked at was nice but not quite right for us, so we hired a contractor to build a house just for us.

Dave had just been placed on the subdivision's approved contractor list, so we got a great deal so he could get started in the new neighborhood. We picked out a nice lot, selected a plan we liked, made a few changes, and construction was underway. Bare dirt to the finished house took about six months. We were finally homeowners in a nice neighborhood.

Sadly, my mom never got to see the new house completed. She was 74 and diabetic but was doing well, living at her house until the last year. We all agreed it was time for her to come and live with us. We had enough space in our three-bedroom apartment, and our daughter loved having my mother around.

Mom got to see the plans for the new house, and she was so excited for us. Unfortunately, she just wasn't able to stay around long enough. Her diabetes had taken a toll on her circulatory system, especially in her legs. She had already been in the hospital twice within a year, and she was back again.

Her doctors said they could add some time to her life if they amputated one of her legs, but Mom was a strong woman until the end. She told them it made no sense to start cutting off parts just to live for another few months. She told them "That wouldn't be living." I still miss her.

By the Fall of 1976, we had been in the new house and neighborhood for about two years. Sandra and I had made it to 31; Elaine was ten, and little Michael was four and growing fast. Sandra and I both stayed very busy, but did our best to carve out time for the children.

Elaine was a cheerleader for her elementary school's football team, and I was taking her to a Saturday morning game. She was so cute in her cheerleading outfit and was actually a good cheerleader. We were not far from the house and approaching an intersection when I noticed Elaine didn't have her seat belt fastened. I reminded her that we never ride without our seatbelts fastened, so she buckled up. As soon as she did, we began our left turn through the intersection when a drunk driver in a pickup truck ran the stop sign and hit our car at full speed. The impact was on the front left, the driver's side of our car.

I don't remember the impact so much as the car roughly bouncing to a standstill about 50 feet up the other road, facing the other direction. I immediately checked Elaine, and she said she was ok. I told her not to move until someone came to help.

I sensed the wreck was bad, but did not realize much else. Our car had landed facing the bright morning sun, and the steam, billowing up from the front of the car, mixed with the sunlight to create a bright, hazy, dreamlike scene.

My face felt wet and gritty to my touch, and I saw shattered glass and blood on my hands. I wanted to get the glass away from my eyes, so I grabbed the black towel that was being used to cover a split in my old seat cover and gently wiped off my face. I draped the towel over my head to block the harsh sunlight and drifted into unconsciousness. I must have been a strange sight for the first people on the scene.

I vaguely remember hearing the sound of people shouting and sirens in the background. I felt calm and unattached to the chaos below me when I woke up. I was floating about twenty feet above the wreck scene, looking down at all the activity. I wasn't afraid; it felt so normal hovering above it all. It was like I belonged there.

Then an incredible sense of peace and serenity came over me as I was bathed in a soft, warm, white glow. The radiant light flowed from a much brighter area higher up and behind me. The light was drawing me, compelling me to come to it. As I turned and began my ascent toward the source of the light, I found the sense of calm, peace, and protection irresistible.

As I drew closer to the brilliant source of the light, I could see it was coming through a large opening, and I was able to make out the faint, backlit images of people gathered just inside, waiting for me, welcoming me.

I could sense an overwhelming spiritual presence wrapping around me and drawing me closer. It seemed as though I was entering heaven. I was almost there; It was so close, peaceful, and wonderful.

Then, just as I approached the opening, I started hearing the distant, distracting, creaking, popping, and grinding sounds of metal being bent and torn.

I remembered the wreck, it seemed so long ago and so far away, but something was happening back at the wreck scene.

In that brief moment of distraction and hesitation, I thought of my daughter, who may have been injured, and the family I was leaving behind. I wanted so much to embrace the light, but I just couldn't do it; I had to go back. The beautiful light quickly grew dimmer in the distance as I descended away from it. As the sounds of bending metal grew louder, I sank into darkness.

I had a short moment of consciousness and realized the noise that had interrupted my journey was coming from the Jaws of Life as the rescue workers used them to pry open my side of the car so they could remove me. The next thing I remember was being placed into the back of an ambulance. I saw my little cheerleader sitting upright in the back of the ambulance. She was going to be fine, and I was alive. The sirens started blaring, and we were on our way to the hospital.

I had been unlucky enough to be involved in a serious auto wreck, but so fortunate to experience an "OBE" triggered by an "NDE." These nice acronyms stand for "out-of-body experience" and "near-death experience."

My versions of these phenomena were right out of the textbooks. My head trauma was followed by unconsciousness and the totally believable sense of hovering above and looking down at the active wreck site. That, and ascending toward a beautiful, welcoming light and having a strong sense of peace and spirituality are classic parts of these events.

It is amazing just how clear and real it seemed at the time. It was so much more believable than a normal dream, and it played out in real-time along with the physical event taking place around me. I can fully understand how some people who have experienced an NDE-OBE are convinced they actually died, went to heaven, and returned.

Elaine sustained some bad seatbelt bruises and a lot of soreness. I suffered a severe concussion and some lacerations on my head. To this day, I can't believe I had no broken bones and walked out of the hospital.

However, by the time I got home, I felt like the left side of my face and neck were sunburned, and the area was somewhat red. Unfortunately, no one noticed it at the hospital, but the truck's battery was crushed in the impact, and some of the battery acid came through my busted window and landed on me. The resulting acid burns left the skin in that area noticeably darker.

On a lighter note, every area where the acid had splattered on my clothing was dissolved when the items were washed, leaving those clothes looking a little like Swiss cheese.

One of the side effects of that concussion, other than the headaches and fatigue, was strong, vivid nightmares. The first one was by far the worst.

I was lying in a tent in the woods and realized something bad was about to get me. I don't remember what it was, but it was bad, and I was frightened. I started to get up and run, but I couldn't move, no matter how hard I tried. I started to scream, but nothing came out. At that point, I was totally terrified and trying my best to scream and run.

Suddenly, I broke free, got up, and ran out of the tent screaming. Evidently, my brain forgot I was asleep and turned off the protective mechanism that normally keeps people from moving much during dreams. I actually started screaming, jumped out of bed, and took off running. It was a very short run. It ended abruptly when I collided with the bedroom wall. I collapsed to the floor against the wall and started crying out of fear and pain.

Poor Sandra and the kids had no idea what was happening, and I didn't either. They were frightened but helped me up from the floor, and we all adjourned to the living room for some much-needed quiet time. It didn't take long to determine what had happened. That nightmare was so vivid and frightening in my mind. It still is today. I could not go back to sleep for fear it would happen again.

After a week, I went back to work. All my fellow workers greeted me, and after about twenty minutes of the Richard's Wreck show, we all went back to our desks. I sat down at my desk and realized I had no idea how to do my job. Using my computer terminal was a complete mystery, and all the program diagrams taped on the wall, the ones I had created, might as well have been a child's daycare drawings because they didn't mean a thing to me.

That realization wasn't as bad as the nightmare, but it really scared me. My mental processes did improve a little every day, and I was much better by the end of the third week. Living through my brain's healing process was a real learning experience. I had no idea just how valuable that lesson would be many years later.

8

Vote for Richard

Maybe it was that hit to my head from the car wreck, I don't know, but I decided to run for public office. Looking back on that decision with insight and honesty, I believe there were two reasons I made that choice. First, I believe most people who run for office do it for the attention and feeling of importance and relevance. I was no exception. And with all due apologies to the majority of people holding elected positions, at one time or another, we all think we can do better than those idiots and crooks.

For several years, I watched our bedroom community grow along with the whole Atlanta area. A city just south of us and a little closer to Atlanta was already much more developed and, in my opinion, a mess. Poor planning had led to ugly, unorganized sprawl and traffic congestion. I did not want that to happen in my little city. I knew I could help if I were on the city council. How hard could it be to get elected? Raise some money, put up some signs and make some speeches; city council, here I come.

I knew I needed to raise some money, and I needed to knock on a lot of doors. Both seemed to be easier than I thought they would be. Several merchants I knew were happy to donate a little cash to my campaign, and thanks to my early experience as a door-to-door brush salesman with the Fuller Brush Company, selling myself door-to-door was easy also. Knock on a door, hand them a brochure, and tell them all the good things I would do when elected. It was going well.

As the election drew closer, the town hall meetings cranked up. This meant it was time to stand in front of a crowd and give a speech. Thankfully, I had recently taken a college elective course called "Speech with Creech," Professor Creech that is. It was a torturous class where we had to create speeches and deliver them in front of the class. I was great talking to friends and terrible talking in a more formal setting in front of strangers. That class really helped. I learned to make bullet point notes to refer to as I talked and to breathe and look at the audience.

My first announcement speech was at a small local auction house where I was a regular at their monthly Saturday night auctions. I had been both a buyer and seller of goods and made a little extra money with it. I was friends with the owner, and he'd let me fill in as the auctioneer when he wanted a break. I got to sit up there, holler in a funny, melodic voice, and control the bidding. It was a lot of fun.

Of course, the night I announced I was running for city council and gave my first little speech, I received loud applause and encouragement. After that, I felt like there was no way I could lose.

That night after my announcement, I met Lee, a gentleman I had seen a few times at the auction. He usually stood in the back of the room, and although he bought a few things sometimes, it seemed he was just there to pass the time. He wished me well. I didn't know it at the time, but months later, he would make me an offer I couldn't refuse.

My third real speech was at a subdivision clubhouse. It was actually packed with people, and each candidate spoke from a little podium in the corner. I was nervous as usual, but I had my notes. I thought I was prepared, but the lights went out halfway through my presentation. Everyone gasped, and a second later, the emergency lights came on. The room had enough light for us to carry on, but not enough to read my notes. Those notes were my security blanket; I depended on them. I actually knew everything I wanted to say, but I had trained myself to rely on those stupid notes. When I couldn't read them, I froze. It was very awkward.

The first thing I learned in my bid to become a city councilman was not to rely on detailed notes when making a speech. What I was taught but did not learn in that public speaking class was to list the bullet points, but be prepared to carry on if the wind takes those notes away or the lights go out.

Another good lesson if you are running for office in a town with a very popular mayor, you better seek their approval before running. It seems the people the incumbent mayor approves most likely will win. I did not seek the mayor's blessing, and I did not win. I didn't come in last either, though.

It was another great learning experience. I learned a lot about how a city government works and how basic campaigns and elections work, and I also learned I was probably not cut out for politics.

By the fall of that year, I had put the election defeat behind me and was pampering my bruised ego by giving myself a few self-congratulations for all the good things I had going on.

My career was moving right along with three promotions since I started working at the school system data center, and to top it all off, I finally earned a college degree.

I graduated in June with a Bachelor of Business Administration degree with a major in finance. That degree came after four years as a full-time night student. I had aimed high and wanted a 4.0-grade point average, but happily settled for a 3.5 average. I went a little easy on myself for missing the 4.0 mark.

After so many years of trying to avoid the inevitable and embarrassing question, "Where did you go to school?" I had an answer. Even better than having that answer was the knowledge that I set a difficult, long-term goal and stuck to it despite every excuse that begged me to quit. I was no longer like a leaf blowing around in the wind. I had direction, purpose, and determination.

Yes, things really were going well, and it felt like I was actually getting somewhere in life, but I still wasn't satisfied. I still was only a technician, a very good one in my opinion, but I wanted more. I really wanted to be in management, and I had a brand-new degree in just that subject.

Convinced I had a lot to contribute if I could work my way into a real management position at the school system, I sat down with my boss—the data center director. I told him my desire to seek a department manager position. I pointed out that I was a good, hard-working problem solver, and I now had a degree in management.

He agreed with everything I said. Then he informed me of a small problem with my plan to advance. "If you want to be in upper management at the school system, you must have a degree in education." "Education?" I didn't want to be a teacher; I wanted to help manage the logistics and business side of the school system. "Sorry, that is a requirement. If you want to be an upper-level manager at the school system, you must have a degree in education."

Well, that certainly explained why the school system seemed so inept and inefficient. I had advanced as far as I could, again.

Soon after that meeting, I was back at the local auction house, and so was Lee. He came right over to me and started asking me about my job. "Didn't you tell me that you work with computers and accounting software?" As soon as I said yes, he started laying out his idea for a business. His family had been in the automotive business, and Lee had a lot of knowledge about automotive dealerships. He explained how auto dealerships were still in the dark ages as far as accounting goes, still pencil and paper for the most part.

Lee was trying to develop a computerized accounting system for auto dealers. He had done some legwork and found a computer manufacturer with a basic accounting package that was affordable, actually free. The local sales office of the Digital Equipment Corporation, a major player in small mainframe computers at the time, had a deal for Lee. If he bought their computer systems, he could have their basic accounting software for free.

Lee's idea was to get the software, modify it to accommodate automotive dealerships' specialized needs, and sell them a ready-to-go hardware and software package that would computerize auto dealers' accounting and basic business data. No companies were offering an affordable package for auto dealers at that time. Lee already had an investor willing to put up money to fund the startup, and he had a computer company with computers and basic accounting software. But what Lee did not have was any idea about computers and software. He needed my help. The winds of my life were starting to blow again.

Lee and I met often after that initial meeting. A plan was emerging. He had access to startup capital, the idea, and knowledge of the auto industry. I had the computer expertise and creativity needed for marketing. Several months later, we formed a new company, Dealer Data. Lee was president, and I was vice president. We came up with a salary that would allow me to survive during the startup period and, of course, a good contract and profit split for the future.

The next National Auto Dealers Association show was coming up in three months, so we had a lot to do to have something to present there. I resigned from my school's system data center job and jumped headfirst into the new business. I named the package "FIDO" for Fast Input Data Organizer, took a picture of Lee's dog, and put the name and the cute dog on promotional t-shirts. Next, we came up with the price points for the various hardware and software combinations and created brochures touting the FIDO system's features, advantages, and benefits. We could get our brochures mailed just before the convention; we were ready. The NADA convention went reasonably well, with dealers showing a lot of curiosity and wanting to learn more. We were pleased with our first step.

After the show, we started working on all the sales leads, and I flew to meet a few of the most interesting prospects. We were reasonably confident we would have our first sale within a month. I spent most of my spare time modifying the software to do the things we said it would. The new venture was looking good. The only thing I was worried about at that time was Lee.

It seemed Lee had some issues that became more apparent as our relationship evolved. Lee was married with two children but separated. He also tended to drink heavily at times and would call me to talk. I felt like his personal psychiatrist sometimes as I listened to his problems.

Lee was also a pilot and had a small two-seat WWII trainer plane he would take up every few weeks. He called me one afternoon in good spirits because we were close to making two sales, and he wanted to celebrate. "Come over, and I'll take you up in the plane for a view of Atlanta at night; it's spectacular." I wanted to say yes, but I needed to spend more time at home with Sandra and the kids. Besides, I just wasn't that comfortable with the thought of flying with Lee in a small plane at night. Since I declined his invitation, he called the investor, and they went up for the joy ride.

Even though he had been drinking, he remembered exactly how to fly the plane; unfortunately, he forgot it needed fuel. The plane went down in a patch of woods not too far from the airport. The investor survived the crash, but Lee and our company did not. It appeared my decision not to meet Lee that evening was a far better one than my decision to go into business with him.

I was shocked and saddened by Lee's death, but the sudden loss of my job and my dream of success, for some reason, didn't bother me. I had been there and done that a few times and believed I would be able to pull another job rabbit out of the hat before we went broke. I wasn't sure Sandra shared my confidence, but I was experienced with what to do when suddenly unemployed. Contact several personnel recruiters and start searching the help wanted ads. The second agency I contacted asked me a few questions and, as they all do, asked me to drop by as soon as I could.

I decided to drop by that afternoon since I no longer had a job and had nothing else to do.

When I met with Don, who operated the small recruiting agency, he asked me a lot of questions as he poured over my resume. He then asked me if I would consider something other than working in the computer field. Since all my great career plans for that field weren't working out so well, I said, of course. Thirty minutes later, I had a new job as a personnel recruiter. Don said he thought I had what it took to be a personnel recruiter, and since I knew many facets of the computer industry, I would be a great addition to his small firm. However, there was one small catch. I would be paid on commission for each job placement I made. I liked that even better. If I worked harder, I would earn more.

Don and I got along great. He took me around to meet his contacts in the companies that placed job orders with his firm. This was not complicated; meet and screen job applicants and match them with the company's job openings. Dress them up, prep them on the company and position they will be applying for, coach them on proper interview techniques, send them out, and get a cut of the fee paid.

At that time in my life, I was not very comfortable dealing with strangers on a personal level. Actually, I could do it, but I didn't like it. Six weeks into that job, I did not have a single one of my candidates get hired, so I earned nothing. My days as a professional job recruiter and a headhunter were over. I went back to being a full-time job seeker. Don did say he would call me if he saw anything I might be interested in. I never really expected to get that call.

The pay I had received from the ill-fated Dealer Data venture was barely enough to get by on, and I had earned absolutely zero as a personnel recruiter. Sandra had been an office worker with one of the large communications companies for a good while, but her income alone was not enough. The Cole household was out of money, we were broke. The stack of unpaid bills and the credit card balance got higher as each week passed. It would be a gross understatement to say things were a little tense at home. It was starting to look like we could lose the house and the new car, but, one more time, and just in time, I got another new job with another small company.

This young company, however, was stable and growing. It had found a niche serving the auto dealer community with small, programmable desktop machines that could calculate monthly auto-loan payments based on selling price, trade-in value, and cost of add-ons like undercoating and insurance.

I had solid programming experience, and because of Lee and Dealer Data. I was now familiar with the needs of auto dealerships. This job was a great match for me. They were happy to find me and named me VP of Sales. I was their first "executive." It was a small company; the "VP" title wasn't that big of a deal, and the pay wasn't a lot, but it was a lot more than nothing. Once again, there was hope for the future.

9

The Talk

As we eased into 1978, our little family looked a lot like the perfect American family, a nice couple in their early thirties with two great kids, new cars, and a new home in a new neighborhood. It was picture-perfect, but pictures don't always show reality.

It was early February of '78 when Sandra decided we needed to talk. "Richard, you need to move out." "What?" "You need to move out," she repeated. "What do you mean I need to move out?" was my stunned reply. "We just can't stay together anymore." Well, she certainly got to the point quickly enough. That little conversation began a hard, tense, gut-wrenching dialog that went on for several days.

Sandra's decision to have "the talk" came during a period of unusually high tension and frustration. She needed a break from "us." I was probably feeling the same but was not ready to acknowledge it. We were both emotionally numb and bewildered that our relationship, our lives, had gotten to that point. We had been married for 13 years, but the perfect little couple wasn't so perfect. We were separating.

A week later, Sandra and I had a calm, informative, but frank discussion with the children. Elaine was already 11 years old, and Michael was only four, so the bulk of our concern was for Elaine's well-being since she had a much better understanding of what was happening. If neither Sandra nor I did anything else right, we did our very best to keep the messy side of the separation out of the children's view and hearing. We also made sure they understood we both loved them very much, and none of our problems were their fault.

I put my clothes, a few personal items, and an old 13-inch, black and white TV with its rabbit ears antenna in the car and went to my new home. It was a small, efficiency apartment close to my new job. I rented a bed and sofa and picked up some basic groceries to get started.

I wasn't much of a drinker, but after the first sleepless night, I picked up a few bottles of cheap wine in hopes that a few drinks at night might help me sleep. I got through the days reasonably well, but the nights were much harder. Tears came much easier than sleep. The first few weeks were the worst. My whole world had turned upside down, and I fell off.

"What had happened?" That was the question playing over and over in my spinning head. It was too bad I couldn't summon up one of my "spontaneous moments of stunning mental clarity." That would have given me answers much quicker, but the answers I needed didn't come quickly or painlessly. Instead, it took a few agonizing weeks for me to sort it all out and clear the fog sufficiently to see what led us to where we were.

The breakup didn't happen because of some specific event or transgression. Our honeymoon was over by the third year, and the romance had been slowly fading since then. Our relationship had become a job, a responsibility, something we were supposed to do. The changes were so gradual, so subtle; I don't believe either of us even realized it was happening until it was too late.

What went wrong? Everything. First, we were so very young when we married. I won't say we were immature, but we were inexperienced in life as adults. We had not reached a point where we really knew ourselves; at least, I hadn't.

Although we seemed to be compatible, we were very different people. Sandra was a calm person who enjoyed cooking and sewing. She was mostly content with her position in life, and there was absolutely nothing wrong with that. Me, well, I'm not a calm person. I am more of a get-up-and-go, chase the next adventure, risk-taker, and there's nothing wrong with that either.

The second problem was the tensions my risk-taking and job changes created. I changed jobs far too often. Sometimes it was my choice, sometimes the employer's choice, and sometimes it was just fate. I always seemed to land on my feet after each employment interruption and we never totally crashed and burned financially. But each job interruption caused another heavy load of uncertainty, insecurity, and stress to get dumped onto our relationship.

Third, what probably had the biggest impact on our relationship was the amount of time I was not at home in the evenings and on weekends.

During several extended periods of our 13 years of marriage, I either worked two jobs or worked a lot of overtime. Then there were the four years of full-time night school, and somewhere during our time together, I squeezed in a year of law school.

I wasn't at home as much as I should have been. It would be convenient to say I was doing it all for the family's good, and I was, in a way, but mostly I was feeding my desire to get ahead in life.

I know this sounds like everything was terrible all the time, but it wasn't. Sandra had her faults, and I had mine, and we each wanted something different out of life. But we also had a lot of good times along the way. And through it all, we never lost respect for each other. Of course, there were disagreements and tensions, but neither of us was ever abusive in any way. I credit both of us for that.

After those first few weeks of being apart, I better understood what had gone wrong. We both could have done more to help the relationship, and I think both of us were still hoping we would be able to get back together after a cooling-off period. In the meantime, I had to adjust to my new environment.

A few months after I moved into my new, very tiny, efficiency apartment, the complex's self-appointed social director dropped by to invite me to the resident's monthly get-together at the clubhouse. Since I was a new resident, she said it would be a great way to meet some other residents.

Only a few people attended that clubhouse social, but one of them invited me to an upcoming birthday party for Sam, whoever that was.

The monthly get-together was a little on the slow side, but evidently, everybody knew Sam, and his 55th birthday party had attracted a large, lively crowd.

For the first fifteen minutes of Sam's party, I was busy with a barrage of hellos, followed by the required "How long have you lived here?" and "Are you married?" questions, followed by "I'll see you around." I wondered if that was normal single-life stuff? I wasn't sure how it worked or what the rules were. I finally got a drink and sat in a corner, watching all the strangers mingle. I didn't mind just watching; I knew how to do that.

Each time I noticed the front door open, I glanced toward it to see who was coming or going. Then I saw her. There seemed to be a warm aura surrounding her as she moved effortlessly from the entrance into the crowded room. She smiled and greeted the other guests like a star greeting her fans. I couldn't keep my eyes off her; I was mesmerized by her presence and her every move.

It was a magic moment when she turned my way, and our eyes met. No words had to be spoken; the moment was electric. She gracefully and purposely moved in my direction as I stood, transfixed by her attention. We both were somehow oblivious to the others in the room; we were alone as we met. We were perfect strangers a moment before, but we embraced as firmly and tenderly as soul mates destined to spend eternity together.

Ok, so that's not exactly how Nancy and I met. But she did come through the door, and I did see her, and yes, I thought she looked nice. She mingled, and I just sat in my corner watching the crowd.

She later told me she came over to talk with me because I was alone. I was, indeed. It seemed so easy talking with her, no pretenses on her part, no come-ons from me, just friendly conversation. A little later, one of us came up with the idea of getting something to eat.

There was a barbeque place not too far away that served food until 1:00 am, so we left the party. We had a midnight snack and a chance to talk without the distractions of a party. I learned that Nancy had come to the party because Emily, who rented a room from Nancy, knew the person throwing the party for Sam, so Emily invited Nancy to meet her there. Emily didn't show up, but Nancy did.

After our midnight snack, we returned to the apartment complex, and I suspect we discussed going on a real date, but I don't remember the details. We said goodbye, and Nancy drove home.

I learned a lot about Nancy as the months rolled by. She was born in Atlanta, Georgia, but her family moved to Charlottesville, Virginia, when she was five. She had two older brothers, and her dad was a postman.

When she graduated from high school, she packed her clothes and moved to Atlanta. She loved her parents and had no problems at home; she just wanted to get out and explore other places. Once in Atlanta, she enrolled in a business training school and soon landed a good clerical job in the main office of a large southeastern bank. Nancy was obviously independent and strong-willed.

She was renting a two-bedroom apartment and subletting the second bedroom when we met. I also noticed Nancy's car wasn't brand new, but she kept that thing spotless inside and out. She was neat and organized; both admirable qualities.

The only problem I could find with Nancy was her age. She was young. I was 33, and she was only 23 and didn't look that old, but Nancy's behavior, self-discipline, and conversations with me reflected a person much more mature than her 23 years.

Actually, there was another problem with Nancy. She was too likable, too good of a fit for my personality, and way too easy and fun to be around. That was a big problem because I did not want to get involved in a serious relationship. I just wasn't ready to do that again.

As the months rolled by, the financial burden of my separation from Sandra was becoming more of a problem. We could not afford our house payment and my apartment's rent and utility payments. Hence, Sandra and I decided that we had no choice but to sell our house. There was no other way to survive the mounting debts. And just as it was logical for me to be the one to move out, it was also logical for me to move back in to get the house ready to sell.

Sandra and the kids moved to an apartment, and I moved back into the house. I cleaned up, touched up, and fixed up everything that would help the house impress a buyer. The house was ready to be put on the market in a few weeks. If we were lucky enough to sell within 60 days and get our price, we would clear just enough to walk away without debts. Sandra had moved, the house was up for sale, and at that point, it was just a waiting game.

While I was living at the house, Nancy came there to spend a Saturday with me. It was well after lunch, and Nancy had put on her bathing suit and settled into a lounge chair on the back deck for a little tanning time while I worked inside.

When I heard a car pull up in front, I thought it was a real estate agent and went to the front door to greet them. But it was Sandra who had decided to just drop by. I don't remember much of the details of that interesting social event, except my wife had just been introduced to a very young, good-looking, petite blond in a bikini on her back porch.

Yeah, that introduction was a little awkward. The visit did not last long or go well. It was tensely civil and courteous, but I had strong suspicions that Sandra was really, really mad. I think the old saying "if looks could kill" sums it up fairly well. I don't believe it had ever entered her mind that I might occasionally spend some time with a female friend, even though we had been separated for quite a while.

The house did sell about a month later, and that allowed us to catch up on the bills and eliminate the large house payments. We had a little financial breathing room for a while. That also meant I had to move again, but that was easy. Sandra already had most of the furniture in her apartment, and I didn't have much at all. My old apartment complex had a full-size one-bedroom unit available, and that was better when the kids stayed with me. I was back "home" again.

Several months after the house sold and I had moved back to an apartment, I received a call from Sandra asking me to meet her for lunch near her workplace. Sandra just said she wanted to talk with me. I guessed it was about the kids and school or the schedule for the kids to stay with me.

We met outside a salad buffet restaurant and went in for lunch. It was a pleasant lunch, but I kept waiting for the "talk to you" subject to come up, but it didn't. Our entire conversation was cordial and light, nothing serious, no complaints to air, and no mention of money, just friendly chatter.

We had finished lunch and walked out to our cars before she finally got to the real reason she wanted to talk. She had been thinking and wondering if I would like to get back together to see if we could make things work out.

I could not believe what I was hearing. I had waited and hoped for that moment for a long time after we had separated more than a year before. My mind started racing as I tried to grasp what she was saying. As she continued, something changed, and I began hearing her words as though she was talking to someone else. I was hearing but not listening.

Another spontaneous moment of stunning mental clarity had begun. Just like my other "moments," the mental fog dissipated, and the reality of the relationship between the two of us was there for me to see.

Instantly and clearly, I finally understood that no matter what Sandra or I wanted, we were totally different people with hopes of holding onto a marriage that was probably doomed from the start and had no chance for a successful future. It was a brief but powerful glimpse of reality. Then, a calmness settled over me, and I knew what I had to tell her.

As I returned from my "moment," Sandra was just looking at me, waiting for a response. I took her hands and thanked her for offering to give the marriage another chance. Then I just told her the truth. I let her know she was a good person and I cared for her deeply, but I knew our relationship would eventually end the same way it did the first time.

I think deep inside, she knew that was true. We talked a little more; I don't remember what about. We shared a warm, meaningful embrace, got in our separate cars, and drove away. The sadness of the moment and the pain of the old memories faded as I realized my decision was hard but best for both of us. I had just shrugged off the past, and it was time to move forward with my life.

A few weeks later, I was served with the divorce papers. Sandra and I met with her attorney, and after some back and forth, we came up with a settlement. When the negotiations were final, I had to give her more than I wanted, and she was getting less than she wanted, so I felt it was a reasonably fair settlement.

As divorces go, that one wasn't at all newsworthy or unique. Personally, it was a major event in my life, and it was not pleasant. But on the other hand, it was a real learning experience on many levels.

10

Moving to Fun Town

Back at the old apartments, I had settled into a good routine. I'd go to work, keep the kids when it was my turn, and get together with Nancy when we could. On one of the weekends when Nancy came over, we heard an old song on the radio but could not remember who sang it. Curiosity drove us to walk up the street to a small music store, looking for the answer to the burning question. The sales clerk on duty had no idea, but he pointed out a man looking at some records and suggested I ask him because he was a musician. That's when Nancy and I met Bill and his wife, Andrea.

They were nice people, and Bill was, in fact, very knowledgeable about songs and artists from the 50s and 60s rock eras. We got our answer, and we learned more about Bill and Andrea. They had a part-time band that played at parties, wedding receptions, and country club events. Bill was a high school music teacher in real life, and Andrea worked at a branch of the bank that Nancy worked for. It was an instant friendship, and they invited us to an upcoming event where they would be playing.

Now, I'm not going to tell you that this band was a well-known, hit-making, touring band; no, they were just a few friends who loved music and were good enough to make a little extra money playing the 50's through 70's hits at local events. However, after going to their performance, my first impression was they played well but needed a little pizzazz, like a nice lighted sign, to make them stand out.

I've never been one to keep my opinions to myself, so I mentioned my idea to Bill, and he said they would love to have one, but fancy signs with your band's name on them are hard to find. He didn't really say that, but we both knew the band could not afford to have a sign company make a custom sign, so I said, "No problem, I'll make one for you," and I went to work.

The band's name was Checkmate, a nice simple name. I thought a large checkerboard pattern with marque lights on the sign's perimeter that would move around like old theater marquee lights would look really good.

The new sign turned out much better than I expected, and the band loved it. The lights would appear to circle left or right and flash in a strobe-like manner if it was turned on and off quickly. The only thing it would not do in that pre-electronic era was run itself.

Since I didn't have a lot of other commitments at the time, they appointed me to be the official sign operator. I connected the sign control unit to a bundle of long wires that allowed me to sit off to the side and control the sign's lights so they would "dance" to the music. It made a great addition to the shows, and I had fun with it.

After attending several practice sessions with the band, I finally noticed the sound mixing board. I started playing with it and realized what it could do. Soundboards, or sound mixers, can change the signals coming from each microphone. They can adjust the volume, the highs and lows, sound tone qualities, and even add neat features like reverberation.

With a soundboard, you can keep the music from drowning out the voices or lower a voice that is too loud for the music. The board can tailor each song and each vocalist, and adjust the overall sound for the particular acoustics of the room you are playing in. A soundboard will only do all those wonderful things if you happen to have a soundboard operator. "Hey Bill, can I do that too?"

I had become the band's official flashing sign operator and soundman. Being in control of the sound was more important than operating the fancy sign. The band was good, but it was better with someone, me, controlling the sound from the front where the audience was. I felt like a real part of the band. I wasn't "in" the band, but I was part of it. That changed when Bill asked me to actually play an instrument. Ok, so it was only a tambourine, but I was officially "playing" in the band, and, before long, they had me "playing" the cowbell and the claves, which are short hardwood sticks that make a distinctive clicking sound when struck together.

While I'm taking a little credit for helping the band, I should mention the dancing chicken. Thanks to me, Checkmate became the first rock band we knew of to have a human-size dancing chicken in their show. Yes, that was me.

Growing up in a very modest home meant I learned to collect anything I found that may be usable in the future. So, when I came across some discarded sheets of lightweight foam rubber padding, I took them home. I had no idea what to do with them, but they were perfectly good and free.

For some unknown reason, I decided to build a chicken suit. Perhaps I had seen the early version of the team mascot for the San Diego Padres, a chicken, or perhaps a bad dream inspired me. Either way, I thought it was a great idea. So, I grabbed the scissors, a felt tip marker, and a bottle of rubber cement and went to work. I made a large head, a nice rounded body with suspenders to hold it up, wings, and two large chicken feet. I spray-painted the body parts white, the beak and feet yellow, and topped the head off with a nice red comb. The top of the chicken reached about seven feet, and that chicken suit actually looked really good.

When I made that silly thing, I had no plan. It was just a fun project. Then the thought came that it would be fun to wear that chicken whenever the band played the old Rockin' Robin song. So that's how Checkmate's "Dancing Chicken" started making guest appearances at the shows. The band would start playing the music for Rockin' Robin and singing "Rockin' Chicken," and the chicken would come out and dance to the music. Everyone loved the chicken; it was a big hit.

At this point, I want to extend my utmost sympathy to anyone who has had to wear a big heavy mascot suit and jump around. Three minutes of dancing inside a large foam chicken was another one of life's memorable experiences.

I must admit I'm not a musician or a great singer, but despite those shortcomings, I was able to have the opportunity to experience being in a band, albeit not a famous band and not as a star. It let me feel what it must be like to be in one of the big-time professional groups. I learned that it looks a lot more glamorous than it really is. It takes a lot of hard work and dedication, but there is an addictive allure to the applause and attention, and if you like music, it's more fun to make it than just listening to it.

I worked with the band as often as possible for about three years. That experience was one of few bright spots in that period of my life.

I had only been back at the apartments for about eight months when my reasonably settled life took another downhill turn. I was laid off at CSA. It was not a convenient time to become unemployed. I'm not sure there ever is.

Not long after losing that job, my car was repossessed. It was a 1977 Pontiac Grand Prix, solid white with a T-top and nice wheels, the last vestige of a better life. The repossession was no surprise; in fact, I thought it would have happened sooner. It seems the finance companies are a little strict about making those car payments.

I caught a break when Bill from the band mentioned his sister-in-law wanted to sell her car. It was an old, faded, lime green, gas-guzzling Ford Fairlane, and no one wanted to buy it. That was one ugly automobile, but it was cheap, running, and I had transportation again.

A month later, I was hired by another small software services company. This one provided programming assistance for companies needing additional help with large programming projects. They were looking for help with business systems design and creating system design documentation to help their clients manage their software development projects. Being well trained to help with their needs, I was just what they were looking for. I jumped into their system design programs and created professional customer support documentation for their largest project.

This was another job with a small struggling company. The pay was not great, but the checks cleared the bank. The only problem was that I had started paying child support which did not leave enough to cover my rent. So, I had to find a way to cut my expenses.

Sometimes, as is often said, when one door closes, another one will open. Trina was a young woman who lived upstairs in my apartment building. She worked at a stock brokerage firm downtown and shared a three-bedroom apartment with two guys. One evening Trina approached me with a very interesting proposition.

One of her roommates was leaving the group when their lease ended the next month. Trina and Randal, her other roommate, wanted to move to another three-bedroom apartment closer to downtown, but they needed another person to share the rent. If I joined them, they would make me a deal on the third, smaller bedroom. Going in together on a three-bedroom would save us a lot on rent and utilities. That proposition would almost cut my rent payments in half, and the location was closer to my new job.

I was not a big fan of having roommates since I had never had roommates before; wife and kids, yes, but roommates, no. But financially, I did not see that I had a choice; I was their new roommate.

As soon as my lease ended on the old apartment, I put my belongings into the big, bright green Ford and moved downtown. The area we moved to was somewhat unique. It is probably a far better area now, so to avoid saying bad things about someone's neighborhood, I'll call it "Fun Town" after an amusement park I went to as a teen.

During the first few weeks I lived in the Fun Town community, I suffered extreme culture shock. I was a well-rounded guy from the suburbs, and I knew many types of people, but I had never been so completely immersed in diversity as I was in Fun Town. My new apartment complex seemed to be the epicenter of a biodiversity experiment gone wild.

I am reminded of the anti-discrimination statements used these days by many employers that go something like "We do not discriminate based on race, creed, color, ethnicity, national origin, religion, sex, sexual orientation, gender expression, age, height, weight, physical or mental ability or marital status." That appeared to be the policy and theme for those apartments, and I could add a few other categories that were not discriminated against, but I'm sure you've got the picture.

In all seriousness, that exposure was an unbelievable learning experience. So many people living in that area were so different from me. Their appearances, behaviors, and beliefs were all over the map. After a while, though, they seemed a lot more normal. The lesson for me was that good, bad, normal or strange, gay, straight, or who knows, they were all people just making their way through this world. Some, like me, had fallen to that socioeconomic level; some had made the climb up to it, and others started there and were stuck by choice or chance. Each of them had a unique reason for being there. "There" was not the bottom of the ladder, but it was a long, long way from suburban middle-class living.

Another big difference between my old environment and Fun Town was the pervasive use of drugs. It seemed most people in the area used "recreational" drugs of some type. Marijuana was cheap, readily available, and the most commonly used drug, but cocaine had become the latest "hip" drug. To have cocaine was a status symbol in Fun Town, and it held the top spot on the social drug ratings.

Unfortunately, the strong euphoric high cocaine delivers comes at a very high cost to many individuals. Cocaine can create a strong physical and psychological dependency in many of its users, and the more they use the drug, the more they want to reach the high they crave. The drugs were one of the main reasons many people became trapped in Fun Town. It isn't easy to achieve higher goals when your daily goal is to get high.

Mostly because of the drugs, there was never a dull moment in the apartments. During any day or night, someone would be moving in or out; some couple would be having an all-out screaming fight, and there would always be a party in one of the buildings.

The police were frequent visitors to our apartments. But one night, events escalated to a whole new level. It had just turned dark when the fun started. I heard what sounded like a wreck, squealing tires, and crunching metal. The noise came from the street on the other side of the complex. Sirens quickly followed that from several directions converging on the area.

I'm not always smart, but I am always curious, so I stepped outside into the apartment courtyard to see what was going on. It was definitely getting exciting; two helicopters swooped into view with searchlights exploring all over the intersection and our buildings. It felt like a lot was going on for a traffic accident.

As the event escalated, it was like a scene from the movies, with dozens of blue lights flashing in the streets and reflecting off every apartment window. People were shouting and running, police radios were blaring, and the constant, unmistakable sound of a hovering helicopter with its searchlight sweeping back and forth added to the chaos.

As if all that wasn't enough action, they threw in four or five gunshots. I was beginning to think standing outside was not a good idea when two uniformed officers and a plainclothes cop rushed up the stairs from the parking lot, ran right past me, across the courtyard, and out the other end.

I had a front-row seat to whatever was going on, and as soon as those policemen passed through the courtyard, another plainclothes officer came running up the stairs and straight over to me. "Hey man, which way did the cops go?" he blurted while panting for breath. Things were getting even better; I was no longer just a bystander; I was helping the cops catch the bad guys. "Across the courtyard, they went that way," I told him as I pointed the way. He huffed out a quick "Thanks man," turned back around, and sprinted off in the opposite direction.

It took a moment for me to process the event that had just taken place. So, the police ran through the courtyard and went out over there, and he came looking for them. I showed him the way, but he ran in the opposite direction. I was starting to see the situation more clearly. Either he didn't understand my perfect directions or, or, oh! Finally, I decided it was time to go inside.

The chaos that permeated the apartments had started as a major drug bust that did not go exactly as planned. The bad guys managed to get outside to their car and attempt a getaway, only to be rammed by a police car at the corner. They bailed out of their car, started shooting, and ran back into the complex.

Despite my inadvertently aiding and abetting one of the suspects, everything ended with all the bad guys in custody and nobody injured. It was another interesting night in Fun Town.

11

The Big Party

Although things in my new neighborhood were somewhat chaotic, things were going great at my new job. I had only been there a few months when the owner came into my office after the others had left. He told me he loved the new project management system I created, and he believed it would make a lot of money for the company. He was very excited and extremely pleased with the work I had done.

He told me two weeks later that they didn't have the funds to continue operating; they were broke. I drove back to the apartment in stunned disbelief again. It was all beginning to seem like some cruel joke. Every time I started making progress and getting back on track, something happened to knock me back down.

While there were occasional interesting and productive days, my life had evolved into an endless stream of boring and wasted days. My latest energized round of calling job recruiters, searching the help-wanted ads, and mailing resumes had only resulted in a new stack of rejection letters.

There were few jobs available and a lot of competition for them. Most employers were looking for candidates whose resumes contained things like "spent the last four years rising through the ranks" of a major corporation. My career path history did not read quite like that.

I was getting more desperate, and I needed to find some type of work, anything to earn some money, so I started applying at convenience stores and gas stations. They wouldn't hire me either. I was overqualified, they would tell me. I sensed they felt that if someone like me was applying for that job, something must be very wrong with them. They may have been right. Several of those employers even told me they knew I would quit as soon as I found a job in my field. They were right about that too. I was down to living on unemployment checks and food stamps. I never felt comfortable receiving or using those handouts, but I did it.

It was so depressing to dwell on my situation and far too easy to focus on anything and everything else. Trina, who was also on her way down, had become a cocktail waitress at a local club. When she got off at 2 am her and some friends, mostly other club workers, would return to the apartment and continue the party. This did not occur so much during the week, but Friday and Saturday nights were different. Far too many times, it was alcohol, marijuana, and cocaine until dawn. These were the kind of spontaneous parties that reminded me of scenes from the movie Animal House, except these people were no longer college-going kids.

Most of those times, I stayed in my little back corner room, most of the time, but too often, I joined the party for a while. It was hard to sleep either way, and I never knew who or what I would find in the living room the next morning.

We never had real parties at our apartment, just people dropping by for a while after work. But there were plenty of organized parties in Fun Town. Trina had been invited to a special party, and she asked me to go with her to check it out because it might be an interesting event. That was an understatement.

It was a party for what is now called the LGBTQ community, and it certainly was an interesting event. The large house was packed.

I had always known and been friends with people of different sexual orientations than mine. I knew them and associated with them in the public world in suburbia. But I wasn't in suburbia anymore. I was in Fun Town at their private party on their turf. They did not have to talk and act with restrictions, and they didn't. They were able to be 100% themselves.

I don't want to sound like anything was wrong with any of those people, well, maybe one or two, but I was very uncomfortable being there. Let me explain. Think about a nudist camp, for example. There is nothing wrong with the people there. They are just us, without clothes, participating in a social environment that most will never experience and would not want to. But the nudists are accustomed to it and go about their camp routines with a sense of normality.

Now think about yourself being abruptly stripped of your clothes and thrust into the midst of that nudist camp. I'm sure it would be a very uncomfortable and awkward experience. You would probably get used to it given a little time, but you would first be hesitant to interact with them. Now imagine a group of nice nudists gathering around you for a special welcoming group hug. I don't know about you, but that would most likely push my panic button.

As the party progressed, my sense of unease subsided. I was far from ready for a group hug, but I had reached a point where I could take in the experience of sights and behaviors radically different from what I was used to.

Trina was much more comfortable there than I was. I did my usual "find a seat in a corner and stay there" routine to limit the chances for unusual social encounters. We had been there for over an hour when I realized it was time. I didn't really want to leave my corner, but I had no choice. It was time to go to the bathroom.

Surprisingly, it was fairly uneventful, winding my way across the crowded room with only one playful "What's your name, big boy" comment. I even stopped for a little while as I passed Trina, who was talking with a woman; I was pretty sure she was not a woman. She, or he, actually looked fairly attractive, and I briefly wondered what "she" looked like without the makeup, wig, and dress.

As I chatted with the two of them, I felt my preconceived boundaries of gender identification becoming a little less firm as an experience from my past popped into my thoughts.

I was just out of high school and attending the Southern Technical Institute. A fraternity comprised of students majoring in electrical engineering held their initiation day, and I joined the club. I don't know why; it just seemed to be the right thing to do at the time.

Part of the initiation required the pledges to dress as females for a day. Our family friends who lived around the corner had a daughter about my size, and she was way too happy to loan me some clothes for my initiation. Dottie and her little sister, Ann, insisted on helping me look just right by showing me how to apply lipstick and eyeliner properly. They laughed the entire time, especially as they fitted me with a stuffed bra.

The next day, I put my "costume" on with a wig, semi-high heels, and a matching purse and carefully applied my makeup as instructed. It was quite a transformation. It wasn't me I saw in the mirror, but whoever it was, they were ready for initiation day at the college.

It actually went well. Since other guys were doing the same thing and everyone knew what was going on, I did not feel too self-conscious. Most of the other guys had just put a dress on over their jeans and added the required lipstick.

I was thankful for Dottie and Ann, whose help got me voted best-looking "girl" pledge on campus. I'm pretty sure I won because of the costume and not my wonderful figure. I was also thankful for years of ice skating, which let me handle the high heels without inflicting any major damage to myself. And, to this day, I'm very thankful there were no smartphones to take pictures.

So, who was I to judge others at the party, since I had also dressed as a woman and went out in public?

I finally slipped an "excuse me" into the conversation with Trina and the "lady" and made it to the bathroom. It was a normal bathroom with a toilet, a tub with a shower curtain, and a small vanity sink. I shut the door, unzipped my pants, and my mind took off on a beeline to paranoia city.

Suddenly, I pictured all sorts of weird and wild people hiding behind that shower curtain. Maybe there were two or more people in there doing weird things in the only private place they could find. Or maybe it was a naked, lumberjack-looking guy with a full beard, a bald head, and bright red lipstick just waiting to jump out of the shower to meet me.

Did you ever try to pee while some stranger was watching you? Well, I was trying, but it wasn't happening. I knew it was stupid, but the sights and events of the evening had gotten into my head. I had to look behind that shower curtain. I did not want to, but I had to. Then I started over-analyzing the situation. Do I just quickly jerk that curtain open, pull it open very slowly, just a bit, just enough to peek inside, and should I announce I'm about to pull it open or just do it? I do tend to overthink things when I'm under stress. I finally chose a combo approach, announced then pulled the curtain open at a normal speed. The result was to be expected. There was absolutely nothing there but my over-hyper imagination.

I realized just how ridiculous my imagination, anxiety, and antics were at that point. I put the toilet lid back down, turned around, and just sat down to collect my thoughts. It started as soon as I did, and I couldn't stop it. Another "Spontaneous Moment of Stunning Mental Clarity" had taken control, and I was rendered incapable of anything but giving it my full attention.

That particular moment of clarity did not present me with a clear vision of my reality and gently let me decide my course of action. No, this one seemed to have an attitude. I felt it was shouting at me like a fed-up parent scolding an unruly kid.

"You have become one sorry excuse of a human being. What do you think you are doing with your life? Remember the steel mill? You were going to spend the rest of your life there, but I spent my precious time and energy kicking your little butt to get you out of there and on your way to a better future. I didn't go to all that trouble just to have you plop your lazy butt down in Fun Town, feeling sorry for yourself, getting high, sleeping late, and wasting your life's precious time. What about the people who love you? Are you going to let them down too?"

I was starting to see my plight and my problems. A string of bad luck and my own poor decisions knocked me down, and I just took it. I had given up the fight. I was like a boxer who is knocked down and begins to think it is much easier and less painful to just lay on the mat rather than struggle to stand back up just to get knocked down again.

It was true; I had given up, allowing myself to become a "used-to-be," a "has-been," living off the welfare handouts, all the while telling myself I was doing the best I could. No, I wasn't doing the best I could; I wasn't doing anything anymore. I was ignoring my reality, the one I didn't want to think about or admit to. I had become a naturalized citizen of Fun Town.

My little moment of mental clarity was abruptly shattered by a loud, harsh BAM, BAM, BAM as someone pounded on the bathroom door. "Everything ok in there?" I replied that I would be right out, took a confirming peek behind the shower curtain, and returned to the party.

I spent the next several days sorting out what my reality really was. I was broke, unemployed, and behind on child support payments. Those things are bad, but things happen in life. I did not willfully create those problems, so I wasn't feeling so guilty about my situation. But I had given up the fight and failed to do everything possible to change things, and that was totally my fault.

My problems not only affected me but also impacted my kids and Nancy. Remember Nancy? We had been dating for almost three years, and for some totally unexplainable reason, she was still there for me. Throughout my long downhill slide, she was there. And the kids, I realized they deserved a better father than what I had become and what I would remain if I did not change my behavior and situation.

It was not easy to face and acknowledge what I needed to do, but that was far easier than actually doing it. I knew it would not be easy, and it would not be quick, but I had to get off the mat and get back in the fight. I had defined a new goal and dredged up the motivation and will to fight back in those few days. I could not surrender to Fun Town.

I started avoiding the parties and the living room's late-night happy hours. Instead, I stayed in my room as much as possible and focused on a renewed job search with a refreshed resume and a renewed determination.

I was totally surprised when I managed to land an interview with Four-Phase Systems, a national computer company. I made sure I got a good night's sleep, made sure I looked as good as possible, and made sure I parked my big, ugly, half-dead, lime green clunker at the far end of the parking lot so no one would see me in that thing.

The interview went well. I felt at ease, and they seemed to like me and the technical experience I could offer. I was very open and honest about my employment history, and I believe they appreciated the honesty. I got a second interview, which went even better than the first.

The company's Atlanta branch was in talks with a neighboring state about computerizing their Medicaid claims processing system. I had the required system design experience, and I was proficient in the computer language they needed. I had finally caught a break. They decided to take a chance on me, and I started my new job the following week.

The Long
Climb Back

It was not easy getting back in the habit of waking up early each day and going off to work, where I faced the learning curve for my new high-tech job, but it sure was a welcome change. The routine of going to work and being away from Fun Town during the days helped me stay away from the drugs and other distractions at the apartments. Things were slowly getting better for me mentally and financially, although it was still a day-by-day challenge with the mental part.

It was going to be a long hard climb up and out of the hole I had gotten in, and there were no shortcuts.

I made it a point to spend as little money as possible as I worked at catching up on priority number one, the child support payments. The next thing I needed to catch up on was transportation. My old car was as close to being non-functional as it could get and still run. I really needed something more reliable since I was assigned to work on that state Medicaid claims processing project, which required me to drive three hundred miles almost every week.

The steady paycheck from my new job was helping me catch up financially, but I still did not have much money saved. So, I started shopping for a really cheap but dependable used car. Those cars proved hard to find because the ones in good mechanical condition were too expensive; it's funny how that works. But my persistence paid off when I found the "Squad Car." It really wasn't a police squad car. It was a basic, four-door, no-frills, pale blue 1975 Plymouth Fury, which the state's Department of Agriculture had used.

Many police departments and other government agencies had used that Plymouth model for years. If you had stuck an antenna on the back and one of those suction cup flashing lights on the dashboard, it would look just like an unmarked police car. But, as I said, it was not a police vehicle, and judging from the scuff marks and animal hairs in the back, it was mostly used in the apprehension of stray farm animals.

The Squad Car had a lot of miles on it, but it was actually in good mechanical condition. It was not ugly, just very plain, but it was also very cheap. I really needed another car, but  there were two big problems. One, I did not have enough money to buy it; and second, I could not get a car loan because my credit rating was about zero at that time.

My well-paying job could have been in jeopardy because my old Ford was ready to die any day, and I had no way to buy another car. I was really getting worried, but Nancy, the woman who had stood by me and put up with me during a long rough period, insisted on helping. I was not comfortable borrowing money from Nancy, but she really wanted to help, and I really needed the help. She simply whipped out her credit card and bought the Squad Car. I was impressed, humbled, and very grateful for her help.

Soon after Nancy bought the Squad Car and put me on an affordable payment plan, she made the last payment on her little yellow Pontiac Sunbird. That gave her a lot more room in her budget, and she was ready to have her own place, one without a roommate. She started the search for a new apartment.

The search wasn't that hard. The Spanish Trace apartments, where I was living when Nancy and I met, were in a great location, had a one-bedroom unit available, and reasonable rents. Being already familiar with the apartments and the neighborhood was an added incentive to move there.

Nancy's new place at my old apartments was small but comfortable. It was a lot better place for us to hang out without any roommates being around. My place down in Fun Town wasn't a great place to hang out; well, it was for the usual crowd, but not so much for me anymore. As the months passed, I spent more and more time at Nancy's place.

Nancy didn't like me living down in Fun Town and would not even go there. I couldn't blame her since I didn't like it either. There was too much drug activity and too many parties, and I didn't need the constant temptations.

It is nearly impossible to stay away from drugs and parties when all your "friends" are constantly engaged in the Fun Town lifestyle. The simple truth; there is only one way to get away from that lifestyle with all its temptations. You have to get completely away from the places and the people. I lived in Fun Town for, well, I don't know exactly how long. A year, a year and a half maybe, the details of that period are a little vague to this day. It was time for me to break that Fun Town spell.

There were four real benefits to Nancy and I living together. First, I was away from the influence of Fun Town; second, I could have the kids come there, and the pool was just across the street. The third reason was the additional savings, sharing a small place, and splitting the rent. The fourth reason was probably the most important. This put Nancy and me into a "living together" situation to see how well we would get along being with each other every day and night. Obviously, we got along great when we were just dating, but living together was very different. Nancy and I had been dating for about three years, and we were entering a much more serious phase in our relationship.

It was really convenient having that pool across the street from our apartment. Nancy and I changed into our swimwear and walked down the stairs across the little street and into the pool. It made for a fun and inexpensive afternoon when I had the kids.

One of the days I had Michael with me at the pool; we had a great time. Michael had just turned ten and was a very active kid, so we played and enjoyed rough-housing in the water. I had thrown Michael a few feet in front of me, and he went under, but did not come back up quickly. I could see his outline through the water, and I bent over to see him better. He blasted up out of the water and straight into my nose, just as I did. I got out of the pool quickly before the blood attracted sharks. Back across the street, I put ice on it. I thought it was broken since it made a muffled crunch sound when we collided.

The swelling wasn't too bad the next day, but it hurt, and it seemed more flexible than it used to be. The young intern who examined me at the hospital and reviewed the x-rays said it wasn't broken but would be sore for a while.

About a week later, I still wasn't convinced my nose was fine. It still hurt, and it would bend in ways it shouldn't, but they said it was fine. The doctor knows best, right? The next day, I received a phone call from the hospital letting me know that they determined my nose was broken in three places after a routine review of the x-rays and diagnosis. I wasn't happy about the failure to catch it the first time. How does someone miss three breaks in one nose? Maybe he lived in Fun Town. I took consolation in knowing I had properly diagnosed my broken nose.

My next doctor visit was to a nose surgeon who went in and put everything back together. To protect his masterful work of art, he covered my nose with what resembled a cast. It was large, thick, and very white. There were strips of white tape radiating out from the cast onto my forehead and cheeks to hold that thing in place. The doctor said he didn't want to take a chance on any of the bones moving until they set. I said I didn't want to take a chance of being seen wearing that thing.

It was bad enough being in the office with everyone looking at my face, but it got worse. My boss told me one of my accounts had computer problems, and national phone tech support could not help them. I needed to fly over there first thing the next morning. That was just wonderful; I was self-conscious enough around my friends and did not want to go out in public. It did not matter what I wanted; the customer wanted me there to fix their computer.

Early the next morning, I walked through Atlanta's huge, crowded airport, checked in at a counter, and got on a plane. Have you ever had a really big pimple on your face and had to talk to someone? They can't help it; they have to stare right at that thing, and even if they aren't, you think they are. Well, the cast and tape were much worse than any pimple I ever had. It looked like I had a large, white crab attached to my face.

You want to get noticed? Just put one of those things on your face and walk around. I kept repeating to myself, "They don't know me, they don't know me, it's ok, they don't know me," but it didn't make me any less self-conscious. I got the computer up and running, and mercifully it was dark by the time I flew back. The darkness helped me feel a little less exposed.

Even without a big white crab on my face, walking around crowded airports has never been high on my list of favorite things to do. It's too crowded, too hectic, and far too noisy. I have always felt more comfortable in the less crowded and less noisy woods. Nancy likes the outdoors as much as I do, so she came up with something interesting for us to do in the woods. She found something to combine our interest in wildlife with our love of the wooded outdoors. One afternoon, she announced, "We were going on a bird-watching walk Saturday morning." "Going on a what?" was my first reaction. I followed that with, "What time in the morning?", followed by, "You're kidding, right?". She wasn't kidding. She thought it would be fun and different to walk in the woods, which we liked, and watch birds, which sounded interesting to her. The local Audubon Society organized the event at a nearby park. Nancy had seen an ad for it and signed us up. She was always finding interesting things for us to do, but I wasn't too sure about that one.

My first thoughts of what that gathering would be like played through my mind. I visualized a group of middle-aged British ladies slowly strolling down a walking path, chatting and stopping here and there to observe the birds. "Oh, look over there, Madeline! I do believe that is a Yellow-Bellied Sapsucker." "My, my, Rachael, you do have a quick eye this morning; it is a Sapsucker. How thrilling, splendid observation. Oh, look at the time. I think we should return to the picnic area for our midmorning tea." "Oh, quite right, Madeline. That will be a nice rest after all this excitement."

Michael was with us that weekend, and he promised not to break any more of my parts. With one old pair of cheap binoculars, the three of us headed off on another adventure. Did I mention the sun wasn't up? I am not a morning person, yet there I was, at the crack of dawn, going to see what that bird-watching thing was all about.

When we arrived at the meeting area, I didn't see the group of well-dressed British ladies, but I did see fifteen or twenty normal-looking people, males and females of all ages. They all had their binoculars, and most of them carried a bird identification book. Other than that, they all looked pretty normal to me.

We split up into two groups, each led by someone who knew what they were doing. A few minutes into the walk, the group stopped as someone quietly informed the others, "Rose-breasted Grosbeak at two o'clock in that bush," and pointed to a bush about forty feet away. My first thought was, why not go back home, get some sleep, have lunch and come back at two o'clock. But, before I said something stupid, I realized that two o'clock was referencing where the bird was in the bush.

I put my binoculars up to my eyes and took a look. There it was, a Rose-breasted Grosbeak, sitting in the large bush at the two o'clock position. Now I was a big nature guy and thought I had seen almost everything that lived in the woods, but this was a bird I had never seen. It was about the size of a Northern Cardinal, but the color pattern was more striking, and the beak was much larger. I was surprised I had never seen one and was impressed by its colors.

I reluctantly handed the binoculars over to Nancy and Michael, who, I thought, kept them entirely too long. I wanted to look at that bird again. It wasn't a rare bird, not even close, but I had never seen one before.

Nancy, Michael, and I had a great time on that bird walk. At one point, a few of us peeled away from the main group and started following a Yellow-billed Cuckoo, and yes, that is a real bird.

There was some excitement that the bird was possibly a Black-billed Cuckoo, only in our area during migration. That would have been a great find, but it would take a much better look to discern the fine details that separate the two species.

As the bird worked its way along a tree line bordering a small stream, it was looking for food. We were trying to keep up with the bird to see it better. The bird finally settled for a moment, and we all got a better look. It was the more common Yellow-billed, but the chase was a lot of fun nonetheless. I was excited because that was another bird I had never seen. I then realized that I had probably seen one several times in the past; I just had never paid close attention to them.

On this walk, I had seen seven or eight wild birds I had never seen before, so I asked one of the walk's leaders how many species there were in Georgia, and he told me there were a little over 400, and over 900 species found in North America," he continued.

My mind took off, crow, robin, pigeon, cardinal, chickens, eagles, and I ran out of names fast, and far short of 400. Add in the new birds I had seen that day, and I wasn't even at 50, much less 400. Where are they? Why haven't I seen them? There were hundreds of wild bird species around me, and I had absolutely no idea there were so many.

The rest of our bird walk was not as fast-paced, but it was very interesting and informative. That event was nothing like I had imagined it would be. It was a lot like hunting with binoculars instead of guns. You move quietly through the woods, searching for prey. When you spot it, you slowly raise your binoculars to your eyes, locate the bird in the field of view, then carefully focus the binoculars until you capture the bird in a sharp, clear image and "got it". You have seen it, identified it, and added the bird to your list. Then the hunt for the next bird begins.

I found the bird-watching thing strangely attractive, and I had to listen to "I told you so." more than a few times.

Seeing a bird through your binoculars and knowing what it is are two very different things. Nancy and I soon purchased some binoculars and a field guide for eastern birds. We had begun learning how to identify the birds we saw around the apartments and on our outings. The old saying "One thing leads to another." is so appropriate here. It wasn't long before we had a small bird feeder hanging from the porch eve of our second-floor apartment. We also put an old pie pan on the porch floor with more birdseed.

We wanted to watch and learn to identify wild birds, so it made sense to put out birdseed and have them come to us. Within a few weeks, birds were coming to our feeder, not a lot of birds, but enough to keep it interesting. There seemed to be three or four types that were the most frequent visitors and a few other species that we saw occasionally.

We enjoyed feeding the birds and learning to identify the different types we saw on our porch. It was not long before we could identify them with just a quick glance. Admittedly, only a few species were showing up, so that wasn't a big accomplishment.

We also found it interesting to observe their behavior. Some would hang out at the feeder, and others would just grab a seed, fly over to a nearby tree to eat their seed, and then come back for another. Some seemed to prefer the hanging feeder, and others fed mostly from the pie pan on the floor.

Since there was no grass under the hanging feeder, only cement, I could see everything the birds dropped or threw out of the feeder. I noticed it because I had to keep that balcony floor clean, and there was always a lot of seed on it. I thought it was strange that so much seed fell out, or was thrown out, of the feeder and wasn't eaten. I was curious. Either the birds were very sloppy eaters, or perhaps they didn't like what I was giving them. A few years later, that observation proved to be much more important than I could ever have imagined.

The chaos in my life had calmed down, and Nancy and I had settled into a nice routine. Going to work, coming home, cooking meals, cleaning the house, washing clothes at the laundry mat, and even feeding birds on the porch. We also threw in an occasional inexpensive night out. Since money was still tight, we liked going to the local $1 movie house and sneaking in a drink and some popcorn under our coats. Those were cheap but fun dates. Of course, we would always do something with the kids when it was my turn to have them. It was great to see that the kids liked Nancy, and she liked them too.

Living with Nancy was turning out to be easy and comfortable. I had already met Nancy's parents a few times, and meeting the parents can be a scary event. But they liked me, and I liked them. Everybody liked everybody. Nancy and I had found a good place in our lives.

Just after Christmas in 1981, Nancy wanted to visit her parents in Virginia. I also wanted to go, but I couldn't take off from work, so Nancy had to go without me. Although she was only gone a week, it seemed much longer. The time apart and the quiet evenings alone allowed me to think about our relationship and where it was going. It had been about three and a half years since we met, and I knew we needed to commit to a permanent relationship or move on with our lives at some point.

I had known other couples who were together for five or more years and never married. I understood the reason. Marriage is a real, meaningful commitment with mental, legal, and, in many instances, financial implications. Part of me always wondered why those couples never married after so many years. Another part of me understood it clearly because I feared that commitment also.

I was stuck in the middle between the fear of getting married again and fear of losing Nancy. We had been together a long time. She was my best friend and a wonderful woman. If I lost her and started looking again, I would want another partner just like her.

I didn't really think Nancy would walk away anytime soon if we didn't get married, and marriage hadn't been a topic we discussed, but if we were meant for each other, we should get married; otherwise, we should both walk away.

There was no need for one of my "moments" where all the answers would come to me in one blast of mental clarity. I had figured this one out all by myself. I loved Nancy, and she loved me. I was willing to risk any possible bad outcome to hold onto her. My mind was made up. I was ready, I was excited and wanted to ask her to marry me, but she wasn't there. I wanted to pick up the phone and call her right then. I think I already mentioned I can be a little compulsive at times. Thankfully, I resisted that urge. The next few days were very long. My mind was racing, and I couldn't wait to see Nancy again.

I don't know exactly how long she had been home before I asked her, but I'm sure it wasn't very long. I'll admit I did have a short moment of panic just before the big question. Was I ready, and what if she said no? I was ready, and she did not say no. She was happy, I was happy, and we were starting a new phase of our lives.

We were married on May 1st, 1982. It was a small but nice wedding. Nancy's parents were there, along with my children, and friends and co-workers of both of us. The catered food was actually good and the wedding cake and groom's cake, chocolate of course, were even better. And what would a wedding be without some good music? It just so happened I knew a great little band that volunteered to play for us.

We were able to take a week off, so we made a swing down into Florida and back. Although I did not take Nancy snake hunting on our honeymoon, we still had a nice getaway to start our new relationship.

13.

The Birdseed
Experiment

There were no ifs, ands, buts, or maybes; Nancy and I were married and had started a whole new relationship. But, if we had looked around and checked carefully, we would have seen the same me, the same her, the same apartment, jobs, cars, and the same birds on the balcony. It would have seemed like nothing had changed at all. Nancy didn't even change her name. We decided it was too much paperwork, and besides, her last name is Makepeace; why would we want to change that.

Although it appeared nothing had changed, it had. Our relationship was no longer informal. Instead, it was certified, legal, and intended to be permanent. With that came a reason to make long-range goals and the plans to achieve them. We were in it for the long haul.

First on the list was finding a way to buy a house. We would need a large down payment, so we needed to raise money. We already had a head start since we closely watched our expenses. Our cars were paid for, we did not eat out a lot, and things like going to the dollar movies kept entertainment expenses in check. Whenever possible, we used coupons for purchases and kept a close eye on electricity use and the thermostat. All of those are small things, but they added up.

Then there was our storage bin rental. When we first moved in together, we put the excess furniture in storage. It was not expensive furniture, but in great condition, and like most people, we did not want to get rid of it at garage sale prices. But after looking at it logically, the monthly storage fees would equal the price of replacing that furniture in about two years. It was like buying our stored furniture again on the installment plan, and we were not even using it. We were not sure when or if we would ever use it. We sold it all, banked the money, and stopped the monthly storage rental payments. We had just eliminated a monthly expense and put money in the bank.

That one exercise showed me the value of looking at the wider picture and making logical decisions based on economics and facts rather than sentiment and maybes. Nancy was already very good at managing expenses, and I learned fast. I was determined to stay on solid financial footing and never repeat the money mistakes I made in the past.

When we started looking for a house, the first thing I noticed was the size of the home loan we could qualify to receive. It was far larger than either of us was comfortable with. It was tempting to go for a nicer place, but we searched for something as inexpensive as possible. We were on our second outing with an agent who had already shown us a few houses, all more than we wanted to pay. The agent kept saying, "But, you're qualified to buy this one."

I think she was trying to make a point when she pulled up in front of a house and said, "I think this one will be in your price range." We were in an older 70's subdivision with small cedar-sided homes.

"One story, three small bedrooms, two small baths, and a two-car garage, all on a slab, so no basement. It's only about 1,300 square feet, and it's a bank-owned foreclosure. So, is this more like what you are looking for?" As we looked up the slightly inclined front yard, I noticed that the house color matched the grass; both were dull brown. The house probably had not been painted since it was built, and it looked much older than it was.

Even from the street, I could see the wooden garage door was sagging badly in its middle. The house, however, did have two bright spots. The front door and the old mailbox, mounted on a slightly bent piece of pipe, were both painted bright blue. We had a good laugh and declined her invitation to go inside. Our search continued.

After a few more outings looking for a house that fit our budget, not the agent's budget, we were thinking it wasn't going to happen anytime soon. But that old, faded brown house with the bright blue front door and matching mailbox kept coming back into our conversations, usually followed by a laugh. Having exhausted all other possibilities, I asked the agent to take us back to look at the ugly brown house. We had nothing to lose.

Based on the outside appearance, we had very low expectations about what that house would look like inside, so we weren't disappointed; in fact, we were somewhat surprised. Yes, it was simple, small, and a little outdated inside, but in good condition. My jack of all trades training was paying off. With a good visual inspection, I was able to determine that the ugly, little house had no major problems, only superficial ugliness. We bought the house. My credit was still not very good, but we were buying below what we qualified for, and we could put up a 10% down payment. Our cost-cutting and saving had paid off; we owned a home.

We were excited and ready to get into our first house when moving day came. The move was relatively uneventful, but one of our friendly squirrels and Fleabag, the cat, managed to make moving a little more memorable for us.

Because we had been feeding the birds on our balcony, I started keeping a small bag of peanuts in the shell to feed the Blue Jays and the occasional squirrel. The jays and the squirrels loved those nuts and soon became comfortable enough to stroll into the apartment a few feet to retrieve the peanuts I had placed on the floor. I kept the bag of peanuts in a corner just inside the sliding door leading onto the small patio; in hindsight, not a good idea.

We also kept the sliding door open a little and the bedroom window wide open during hot days to save on air conditioning costs. The door and window had screens so that the bugs couldn't get inside. Since we were on the second floor, we did not worry about people getting into the apartment.

When we got home one afternoon, we noticed that the bag of peanuts had been opened, and many empty shells were scattered about. A squirrel had chewed through the sliding door screen and got into the peanuts. We also noticed several uneaten peanuts beside the legs of the sofa and in corners. The squirrel was storing them for later. Then we noticed that items from our bedroom closet shelf were on the floor, and there was an exit hole in the bedroom window screen.

We believed the squirrel spent most of the day eating and hiding the nuts. It either got spooked or just lost, panicked, and tried to escape through the closet, pushing things off the top shelf before finally chewing its way out through the bedroom window screen. We cleaned up the mess and repaired the screens. On moving day, we found more of the squirrel's stash behind a dresser and tucked neatly into several other places. We had a good laugh.

Fleabag was the name we gave to a sad old cat we saw hanging out near our door. It came right over to me, and I gave it a little scratch on its head. It was a very friendly cat that seemed to like the attention. Fleabag, however, was covered with fleas. Fleabag lived a few buildings away, and it appeared the owner wasn't taking care of it. Fleabag received a good bath and a flea treatment that evening. For a cat, it took that process rather well. Fleabag was a regular visitor at our apartment after that.

On moving day, the cat dropped by and seemed to notice that most of the furniture was going outside and into a truck. Not long after Fleabag showed up, one of the movers called us to the bedroom. The cat had attached itself to the middle of the bare mattress and wasn't moving. The mover tried to shoo it away and even started sliding the mattress off the box springs, but the cat wouldn't budge.

Now I would never assume I know what animals are really thinking, but I suspect Fleabag knew we were moving out and was trying to stop us. I separated the cat from the mattress, one claw at a time so that the movers could do their job. I took Fleabag outside, where we had a long talk. I gave him a final head scratch, and he slowly walked away. Neither of us were happy about it.

We did not have a lot of furniture and junk, so it didn't take long for us to settle into the new place, and then it was time to tackle the "minor" repairs list. That list had grown much larger since we moved in, but the sagging garage door was still number one on the list. Not only was that door ugly and falling apart, it was also facing the street for all to see.

There were four horizontal sections to that garage door. The top two were in good shape since they were more protected from the rain and sun. I planned to remove the two lower panels, disassemble them, straighten them, and glue and screw them back together. As soon as I had the door apart, I realized the lower sections were too far gone to salvage. I thought we would need to buy a new door when I caught a break. A neighbor down the street was installing a new garage door and had piled the old one out by the curb. It was like ours, and he was happy to let me take two good sections off his old door to repair ours. That was perfect timing. The door was functional, looked good, and, best of all, it was free.

Next on the list was the house's exterior, and once I repaired all the loose and damaged cedar siding, it was time for a long-overdue paint job. We were totally surprised at how much better that old house looked with a fresh coat of paint.

A new mailbox and wood post completed phase one of the renovation. As the months rolled by, we cleaned up the yard and got a nice lawn started. Next, the inside of the house was thoroughly cleaned, and the rooms got painted, one room at a time, in our spare time. The renovations were hard work but not very expensive since we did everything ourselves.

As our renovation work wound down, we devoted a little more time to feeding the wild birds. We saw many more birds at the house than we did at the apartments, and that made sense. There were wooded areas scattered throughout the area, and most of the homes had mature trees and bushes.

What didn't make sense was why the birds threw out a lot of the seed from the feeders. I had noticed the same behavior at the old apartment. I never hold back my curiosity, so I decided to figure out what was going on.

I took a ten-pound bag of the birdseed I was using and separated the mix into its components; easier said than done. With the help of a colander, a strainer, and a lot of selective herding with a table knife, I put each type of seed in its own bag. First, I weighed each type to find its percentage by weight of the whole bag. The next phase was the taste test, where I put equal measures of each ingredient into small hanging feeders and small pans on the ground. Then, each afternoon I measured them again and noted what had been eaten. There were four seed types in the bag: sunflower seed, white millet, red millet, and milo, the seed from sorghum cane, a favorite food for doves, wild turkeys, pheasants, and not much else.

The results were just a more scientific and accurate version of what I had noticed on my old apartment porch. The sunflower was always gone every day from the feeder and the pan. The white millet was down a little from the feeder and about one-third from the pan. The red millet and the milo never left the feeders, and only trace amounts were missing from the pans. Most of that was lost from being scattered out of their pans and onto the ground.

I backed up my little sampling project with a trip to the library to do a little research.

The library gods were good to me that day, and I found several references to the birdseed preference tests that had already been conducted. One of them was actually a well-controlled, proper study, and it confirmed what I had learned from my testing. Birds that normally feed above ground level in bushes and trees tend to visit hanging bird feeders and prefer sunflower seeds. Birds that feed at ground level, like doves, will eat more millet, milo, and cracked corn.

What had I learned? The seed most favored by the birds was the sunflower seed. My experiments showed that shelled sunflower, usually called sunflower meats or hearts, was by far the most attractive to the widest variety of wild birds. But sunflower seeds, in any form, were at the bottom of the ingredients list of most commercial birdseed products.

Although that made no sense to me, I understood the reasons for it. First, sunflower is expensive compared to the other seeds, and birdseed was viewed as a commodity, the cheaper the better. Second, it appeared to me, the birdseed company either did not know about the bird's seed preferences or did not care.

I didn't spend much time analyzing why the commercial birdseed was the way it was; I just decided to make my own. My first stop was a local feed and seed store, where I bought a fifty-pound bag of sunflower seeds and a smaller bag of shelled sunflower meats. My crude blend of mostly sunflower seeds, sunflower meats, and just a little millet seemed to be a hit with the birds, and very little of it would go uneaten. I learned a lot, and feeding the birds became a serious hobby for Nancy and me.

Overall, Nancy and I were making great progress. The house was finally in good shape; the yard was looking better than the others on our street, and our birds, showing up in increasing numbers, seemed to be pleased with the new menu options.

Things were even looking good at work. Motorola Inc. purchased Four-Phase Systems, and that really improved my job stability. A bonus was the move to a larger and nicer office building. Our department was expanding, and it was announced that a manager position would be created to help coordinate all the software service work. Another pay grade up the corporate ladder would be great, and I felt my chances of getting the promotion were extremely good. I was their go-to guy for tough computer system problems and the only analyst assigned to design systems and write programs for large clients.

About three weeks later, I was called to the front office to get my promotion. Although I thought that was why they called me in, it was to tell me they were bringing in some guy from the Chicago office to fill the new manager position.

To cheer me up, I was assured that they really needed my technical skills in the field. They also asked me to help the new guy, my new manager, until he was up to speed in my new, I mean, his new position. I wasn't happy about not getting the promotion, but I put it behind me and did my job. I had realized it wasn't the new guy's fault he got the promotion instead of me. It's funny how things work out sometimes; he and I became really good friends.

After the promotion rejection, I put my life back on autopilot, and I still found the job enjoyable. But some annoying little thoughts were moving around in the back of my mind, almost obscured by the ever-present fog of daily life. What was wrong with me? Why do I start a new job, rapidly rise to a position as their best technician, and then watch my career stall at that level? Why couldn't I get to be the person in the big corner office? Why can't I advance into management? Those questions lingered in my mind's background, but I was really good at ignoring them.

I was at my small workbench in the garage, piddling with some minor repair job, when those haunting questions started emerging from the shadows into the bright light of my consciousness. My insecurities and self-doubts were ramping up. "What's wrong with me? I'm a failure. I try so hard, work so hard, but I always get stuck at this level. It happened at the phone company, at the school system, and now it's happening again. What am I doing wrong? Maybe I'm just not good enough. There must be something wrong with me."

My anguish and depression brought me to the point of tears as those repressed doubts boiled over in my head. Then a familiar calmness wrapped around me like the embrace of an old friend.

14

Midlife Crisis

My last "Moment" had seemed to scold me like an angry parent, but this one felt comforting, caring, and wise. It came on like the combination of a benevolent old priest and an inspirational athletics coach.

The rush of clear, honest thoughts flowed in. "There is nothing wrong with you. You have these problems because you are not doing what you were meant to do in life. You have not been, and never will be, successful trying to climb the corporate ladders because you lack the social and political skills required by those career paths. But you have other skills and talents that would serve you well running your own business and being your own boss. That is what you were meant to do. That is where you will find success."

I felt a change in the intensity of the thoughts rushing through my head, as though they were coming from a fired-up, tough love coach screaming his message at me. "You have been training for this your entire life. You have the skills, drive, and dedication for this challenge. You don't need a regimented corporate career. You need to start your own business and do things your way. Create your own career path, and don't let anything stop you; just get out there and do it!"

I wasn't so happy about recognizing I lacked the social and political skills required for corporate advancement, but another concise, clear, and probably accurate insight had been delivered.

I finally understood my problem. I just wasn't cut out for the corporate structure, and I needed to start my own business. There was nothing wrong with me. I just needed to start down a new path like I had done a few times before. Just start my own business; the business will grow, and I'll be successful. That's all I needed to do, start a business.

It didn't take long for the euphoria of my "moment" to fade into a reality check. Starting my own business was certainly not a novel or unique plan, not even close. In the corporate world, everyone, and I mean everyone, was thinking and dreaming of doing just that. So, where was my special, custom-tailored plan for success, my unique roadmap to a better life? It looked like my stunning mental clarity wasn't seeing anything different from what everyone else was seeing; "start your own business." At least I didn't pay anything for that great advice.

After that message from the "moment" had played through my head a few hundred times, I finally got it. I finally understood! "Get out there and do it" was the unique part of the message for me. That was my directive. Get out there and do it. Unlike everyone else, don't just talk about it, don't just dream about it, don't wish it would happen, don't wait for encouragement, don't wait to get started, don't make excuses, and with all due credit to Nike, just do it.

I felt a burden had been lifted from me. I had a new directive, a new goal to take my career in another direction. It felt like I had been suffering from some undiagnosed malady for a long time, and a doctor finally diagnosed my condition and said it was treatable. Of course, I was not cured, but I finally knew what to do. It was a good feeling.

In earlier years, there would have been no hesitation on my part. I would have charged off in that new direction immediately. But it was no longer those earlier years. I was about to turn forty, the big "four-0", halfway between twenty and sixty, and my clock was ticking loudly. I was in a hurry to reach a higher level of achievement in my life.

At that time, my achievements were far behind my aspirations. Fortunately, my age had earned me some degree of common sense, and I knew it would not be wise to quit my job and run blindly in a new direction. My desire to make a complete career change was tempered, but not quashed, by maturity, which was good.

My everyday routines did not change, get up, work, come home, cook, clean, cut grass, etc. All the basics remained the same, but my thoughts were in high gear and focused on starting a business. My first challenge was to determine what business to start. "Start a business" is not very specific, and there are an infinite number of choices in that category. It was an automatic and necessary reflex to narrow the choices to things I knew about or liked.

Bingo, I had it! Both Nancy and I had come to enjoy having the wild birds around. Putting out bird feeders and birdhouses and watching the birds became a very enjoyable hobby. So that decision wasn't so hard. The wild bird thing. I liked it and knew something about it.

After more focused thought, I narrowed my new business down to making birdhouses. I decided to design, construct and sell birdhouses. Building birdhouses as a business wouldn't take much time or money to get started. But, as my brain raced ahead, I realized I needed to develop a better birdhouse to differentiate my product from all the others already on the market. That thought caught me by surprise. I repeated it aloud, "Differentiate my product", yes, my college marketing courses were finally paying dividends.

I soon had sketched out some basic plans for a normal bluebird house and a version that would collapse flat to save on shipping. The collapsible house was more unique, so I went with that design. I decided to use thick western cedar and plated wood screws for quality. It would have the ability to easily shift from its flat shipping position to a sturdy, full-sized birdhouse. The plan was on paper; I just needed to build a few prototypes.

I purchased a small stack of boards in various widths, set up my saw, and made a cut. Well, even good carpenters like myself make the wrong cut occasionally. What my plan showed and what I marked on the wood were not the same. The two side pieces were not right, so I tossed those pieces into the corner and started over. I had smartly anticipated making a few small mistakes and bought extra boards. I quit for the evening. Tomorrow was another day.

The next evening, fresh and ready, I started over, but I made the same mistake again. I threw more wood onto the scrap pile and began my third construction attempt. I was hoping the third time would be the charm, as they say. I measured and cut the side pieces correctly, then incorrectly cut the new roof and floor parts. I ran out of wood with nothing to show but a stack of small oblong cedar rectangles that were, at that point, worthless.

Something was wrong. Evidently, I wasn't focused on what I was doing. Instead, I was making one amateur error after another. Depression was creeping up on me as I struggled to excuse the string of stupid, careless mistakes. I leaned back against the workbench and stared at the pile of butchered planks; I started thinking my great "start a business" plan, like that pile of wood, was pretty much scrap.

I was still standing at the workbench when another "moment" came to my rescue, and I immediately knew what type of business to start. That "moment" was more like a really good "Aha!" moment, quick and to the point. It let me see the obvious, and I felt incredibly stupid for not realizing it much earlier. Birdseed was the answer, not birdhouse. Birdseed was the product to build my business around. That little corrective "moment" got me back on the right path.

There certainly were advantages to going with birdseed. I had already developed several seed blends for my birds, and I knew my birdseed attracted more birds than anything found in the retail stores. I even had a few friends at work and a few neighbors that I had given samples of my birdseed, and they saw more birds at their feeders and were asking me for more of my birdseed.

So, someone other than myself really liked the product. And unlike birdhouses, which can last for many years, birdseed is a consumable product that is used up rapidly and would generate frequent repeat sales.

As I ran the wild birdseed business concept through my head, several glaring problems became apparent. First, mixing and bagging equipment was extremely expensive, making startup costs prohibitively high. Also, I would not be able to buy the bulk seed ingredients in the quantities it would take to get a decent price break. That would make it impossible to turn a profit.

Then there was the competition. Most wild birdseed was produced by a few very large companies that dominated the market. They sold birdseed as a price-sensitive commodity; the cheaper, the better. The retailers, in turn, sold it the same way, "stack it high and let it fly," "ours is cheaper than theirs." I could see no way to produce my seed products as cheaply as most birdseed was being sold in retail stores. It did not appear there was any way for a tiny independent company to survive making wild birdseed.

Even though my analysis of the birdseed venture showed numerous major problems, I still felt I could find ways to succeed. So, I ignored all the downsides of the birdseed business and decided I wanted to start a birdseed business.

"Midlife crisis" is a phrase I grew up hearing. It was usually depicted by an older man driving around in his brand-new red convertible sports car with the top-down and a young blonde, casting adoring glances his way, riding in the passenger seat. Excuse me while I replay that thought a few times. Yes, I can almost feel the wind blowing through my hair and imagine the envious looks from my friends as I slowly drive by. Actually, I always felt a little sorry for that guy. He seemed to be struggling to reclaim his lost youth, which had been left far, far behind as he sped through his middle years.

I was in my forties and on the front edge of my mid-life crisis. I just didn't recognize it. But I wasn't looking for my lost youth; I was looking for the success I always wanted but never had. The old man in the red sports car and I were both chasing something we didn't have. Looking back, I'm convinced chasing my lost youth in a red sports car would have been so much easier than the quest I had started.

By 1985 I was using every spare moment thinking, learning, and planning how to get the new business started. I kept going over and over the known problems: First, seed mixing and packaging equipment would cost more than my house. Second, I could not buy seed in large enough quantities to get decent price discounts, and even if I could buy large quantities, I had no place to store them. Problems one and two made it very clear there was no way I could make a profit. And, if I could get past those problems, problem number three would be waiting. It would be almost impossible to get my new products into retail stores.

On the positive side, we were selling our seed to a few people, although at a small loss, and they really liked it. Even better, they were telling others about it. At that point, it wasn't a real business or even a real product. We were just having fun with it.

We had started putting the seed in old newspaper delivery bags because they were free. A twist tie closed the top, and hand-drawn "For the Birds" labels were stuck on the front. We were only selling a bag or two a week, but the feedback was encouraging.

It's funny how small, seemingly insignificant little things can have a large impact on you at a later time. While wrestling with my dilemma of the high production cost and subsequent higher retail price of my seed products, I recalled my first encounter with Orville Redenbacher's popcorn in the early 1970s.

I was in a grocery store looking at popcorn to make at home, and back then, the popcorn market was dominated by Jolly Time popping corn in plastic bags, and it was cheap. I don't remember the exact prices, but the one-pound bag was selling for about 69¢ a bag. The small 8-ounce jars of

Orville Redenbacher's popping corn were priced at $1.49 and were sitting next to those large, cheap bags of Jolly Time.

Those jars were one-half the size and twice the price of the competition. I bought my regular bag and wondered why Orville's product was so expensive. I also wondered who would buy that little jar at that high price. But, every time I went back to the grocery store, I would see those expensive little jars of popping corn. Finally, in a moment of weakness, my curiosity got me. I splurged and bought that jar of Orville Redenbacher's product.

When I tried it, I was so surprised at how much better it was. It popped up larger and was more flavorful. Although Orville Redenbacher's product was much more expensive, I kept buying it because it was so much better. I couldn't go back to the cheap stuff.

Recalling that experience and realizing that many people, myself included, would pay more for a better product, I became a little less concerned about my product's higher cost. I knew my product would be much better than the competition, and customers could justify a higher price.

There comes a point in creating any new business where you need to have cautious optimism. If you don't have the optimism that your plan will work, you will invest too little time and money and proceed too slowly or not at all. On the other hand, you risk proceeding too quickly without a healthy degree of caution, which often leads to operating expenses outpacing revenue. One way, the business never gets going, and the other way, it opens big and dies quickly.

We had arrived at the point where we needed to do it or forget it. We decided to go for it, but proceeded optimistically cautious. Not too fast and not too slow. I like to think we showed mature restraint and sound business judgment moving forward at the pace we did, but we had no choice. With little discretionary income, very little savings, and our full-time jobs leaving little free time, slowly was the only way we could go. The phrase "starting from scratch" got mentioned more than once.

While handwritten labels and twist-tied newspaper bags were fine for friends and neighbors, it was time to get serious and make the products look legit. We needed real plastic bags and professional labels to have a chance for any sales beyond our friends. The product needed to look like it belonged on a store shelf. I designed some simple but nice-looking labels showing the "For the Birds" logo and the product names for each of the five seed products we decided to start with.

A local printer was nice enough to run a small quantity of the bag labels for a great price. I think he felt sorry for us.

I located a local company that stocked clear plastic bags in the sizes we needed. The bags were relatively inexpensive and ready to fill. However, since twist tying the bags was out of the question, we had to find a machine to seal the bags' open ends after they were filled. I located a really old commercial plastic bag sealer. It was at least forty years old and looked like an industrial-strength "seal a meal," but it was cheap, and it worked.

We had nice labels, commercial-grade plastic bags, and the antique bag sealer, but we still needed a way to mix more than one bag of seed at a time. I tried putting fifty pounds of seed ingredients into a metal trash can and mixing it by hand. Although I could do it and it was a great exercise, that method was too slow and difficult.

Then another one of my great ideas popped up. Just get one of those small, home-use cement mixers. If those things could mix a wheelbarrow load of cement, it surely could mix a little bit of birdseed. The next day I picked up a cement mixer on sale at the local home improvement store and hauled it home. I loaded that thing up and flipped the switch. As the big drum turned around and around, the seed was tumbling over and over, and I was thinking how much easier that was. All I would have to do is stop the mixer and pull down on the lever to dump the mix into the trash can, then scoop it out into the bags.

When the mixer stopped, and I looked inside, the seed didn't look very mixed. It seems that the small round seeds all settled down to the bottom of the batch as the larger sunflower seeds tended to hover on the top. I tried several batches, and each came out about the same. I moved the mixer into a corner and started working on a plan "B."

Plan "B" turned out to be simple, cheap, and effective, although not very efficient. I decided to mix the seed the same way I did for one bag. I would pour all the ingredients for one bag of seed into one bucket, mix it by hand, and pour it into one bag. But this time, I would mix twenty bags worth at a time. I bought twenty small plastic wastebaskets like those found in most offices.

The office trash containers each held enough seed to make the five and ten-pound sizes and still have enough room to give the seed a little mixing with my hands. To measure the seed into the wastebaskets, I found several sizes of metal coffee cans and marked each with a line showing the level for the amount of seed I needed.

Next, I would put an ingredient into a large pail and walk along the line of wastebaskets, dropping the appropriate amount of that seed into each wastebasket. With a few passes down the line, I had ten or twenty baskets filled with the contents needed for each bag. After a quick stir with my hands, the next step was to get the contents of those baskets into a bag and seal it.

Pouring the seed into the bags proved to be harder than it looked. Nancy and I tried several techniques, and none worked well. We needed a giant funnel to guide the birdseed into the bags, so I built a tall wood stand and attached pieces of home heating duct pipe to form a large funnel. It worked great. Nancy would position a bag over the down-pointing small end of the duct pipe and say, "go." I would then dump the wastebasket of birdseed into the large upturned end of the duct pipe, which guided every seed into Nancy's bag.

After all the bags were filled, we would move over to the bag sealer and complete the process by sealing the bags. It was a slow, labor-intensive process, but we could produce professional-looking products without spending much money.

Within a few months, we gained a handful of new customers from referrals by current customers. They all liked our birdseed products, and the new professional look had a huge impact. The seed looked as good as it performed, and customers told their friends.

As we picked up more seed customers, we started getting more questions about which bird feeders they should buy. By that time, I had tried all the feeders found in local stores and knew which ones worked best. After helping many customers choose the best feeder to buy, I realized I should be the one selling them.

It became clear that I needed a way to put product pictures of our birdseed and feeders in front of these customers. In the days before the internet, that meant creating a printed catalog. It took a while, but I finally collected the images of the products I wanted to put in the catalog.

Most of the items we were selling came from small businesses, and they were glad to help us get started, even with my dinky little orders. The print shop that helped me with the birdseed labels also helped me with the first mail-order catalog. It wasn't a slick color production, but it had a casual, personable look and was affordable to create.

For the Birds, Inc. had become a real company, a very small but real company. Its growth was also small, but it grew a little every month. Packaging the birdseed had taken over half of our garage and we had

Nancy working in the bedroom office

started using a small spare bedroom as an office and warehouse for the catalog products. Nancy and I bagged the birdseed a few nights each week and used the weekends to pack catalog orders and drive around to make local deliveries.

It was probably a good thing that For the Birds grew so slowly because money and our available time were scarce commodities. We were operating on a break-even basis and putting our spare cash into more feeder and seed inventory.

By late 1985 we were using just enough bulk birdseed to begin purchasing it from a small local distributor. That meant we got a little better price on the seed but had to buy it in larger quantities. The minimum order to get the seed delivered was 1,000 pounds, which came in twenty fifty-pound bags. That really wasn't a large order, but it was huge for us.

I decided it was too risky to have it delivered to the house while we were at work because it could be ruined by rain, attacked by squirrels, or even stolen. So, I had it dropped off at work to put it all in the trusty old squad car for the trip home.

Because my cubicle office was next to a fourth-floor window, I could see the delivery truck when it pulled into the parking lot on delivery day. When it arrived, I went down and pulled the car up to the truck, and we started putting the fifty-pound bags into the car. You know, "twenty 50 lb. bags" of bulk bird seed is not a lot, until you start stuffing them into a sedan. After a few trial and error starts, and a few pauses for head-scratching, we got every bag into that car. I believe there were six in the trunk, ten in the back seat area, and four riding upfront with me. Getting those bags into that car was a geometric masterpiece. I wrote the man a big check and went back up to the offices.

Several of my coworkers were waiting for me when I walked back into the office. It was like a little surprise party. A few of them were clapping, and all were laughing. Of course, they were kidding me about witnessing the biggest drug deal they had ever seen as it went down in the parking lot. An unmarked truck had pulled up and loaded a half-ton of plain brown bags into my car.

Another friend joked that I had converted my car into a "low rider' because the old squad car was sitting very low to the ground. The thousand pounds of extra weight had overwhelmed the old car's suspension.

That was the first of many seed deliveries, but only a few more took place in the parking lot. After that, I arranged for deliveries to our house early in the morning before work. That saved me from handling those bags twice, and it was a lot easier on my old car.

While we were still not selling large amounts of our For the Birds seed, the little business grew. Every passing month saw a few more new customers and a steady increase in our sales. We were also spending more time bagging birdseed in the garage and making the local deliveries. Nancy's car was newer and better looking than the squad car, so we always used it to make our deliveries. I didn't think my old car would give customers a good impression of us and the business. Besides, we knew that any day could be the day the Squad Car would stop in the middle of the street, belch out a final puff of smoke, and just fall apart.

Corporate Whiplash

With the old squad car about to die any day and the growing business soaking up all our extra cash, I did not know how we were going to replace that car if it died. Sometimes things do work out well, and a little luck comes your way. Motorola finally completed its acquisition of Four-Phase. The old Four-Phase signs came down, and the new Motorola signs went up. We were officially Motorola, and the new business cards said so. The best part was that all the computer technicians who traveled the area received a new company car. I got a nice new Chevrolet Celebrity, and I was one happy employee.

I had entered another period where my life was on cruise control, which was all right by me. There were no traumatic events, personal dramas, and chaotic upheavals to our status quo. That's not to say there weren't some adventures to keep things interesting, and one of those adventures occurred early on a Tuesday morning in March of 1986. It was a typical weekday morning routine with Nancy getting ready for work. She still worked downtown and had to leave earlier than me. I was still asleep since my commute was much shorter than hers, which was good because I don't do mornings very well.

My extra sleep was cut short by Nancy shaking the bed and screaming, "There's something wrong, wake up, wake up, there's something wrong!" I am a sound sleeper, but Nancy's screaming and jumping on the bed did manage to shock me out of my peaceful slumber. The wind was pretty loud, and there was a muffled background sound like constant thunderclaps, but those noises were dissipating rapidly as I sat up in bed.

"What's wrong?" I blurted out. "The house was shaking; something is wrong; it was shaking!" she repeated in a panic-tinged voice. She was frightened, and Nancy was not the scaredy-cat type.

By then, the noise was gone. "It's ok, it's over," I told her to wait there, and I would check outside. I mumbled, "it's ok," again as I went into our front bedroom office to look outside. It was just getting light outside, but everything looked good to me other than something that looked like a large piece of cardboard in the front yard. "It was just a passing thunderstorm; it's gone now." I gave her a reassuring hug and got back in bed. Nancy, on my reassurance, continued getting ready for work.

My sleep was interrupted again about fifteen minutes later by the sounds of sirens outside on our street. When I looked out again, I could see the flashing lights of several emergency vehicles and could hear more in the distance. I quickly threw on some clothes, opened the front door, and went to push open the glass outer door, but it wasn't there. That got my attention. Everything started making sense as I looked both ways down the street. There had been a tornado. Debris was everywhere. The street and yards were strewn with large pieces of roofing, broken lumber, and damaged trees.

It was an eerie sight. There was no panic. Many of the neighbors were just standing in front of their homes, trying to take in what had just happened. More emergency vehicles were coming into the subdivision as police, firefighters, and neighbors checked all the houses, concentrating on the severely damaged homes.

I was so distracted by the scene I had not looked back at my own house. I was a little hesitant to turn around, but when I did look, I was relieved to see the house was fine. The glass outer door was missing, but there was no other noticeable damage. The large and stately pine tree in front of the house wasn't missing any of its limbs, and not a single roofing shingle was gone from the house. And as I approached the house, I saw my glass door lying behind some bushes, fully intact, with only slightly bent hinges. More importantly, no one on our street was seriously injured.

Nancy and I were so fortunate. There was major damage all around us, and yet we were fine. I did, however, have to listen to Nancy tease me for years about sleeping through a tornado.

It did seem good luck, and bad luck tends to even out over time. And while the tornado skipped over us, Mother Nature realized she had missed a spot and decided to come back and take care of the oversight.

Just a few months later it was mid-summer, hot, humid, and perfect for big thunderstorms. The tremendous boom and bright flash really scared both of us. Immediately after the lightning hit, we could hear the hissing and crackling of the electricity as the surge dissipated throughout the house. After turning off the microwave, which had started itself, I quickly checked the attic and each room for any signs of smoke or flames. When I went outside to check the house's exterior, it was easy to tell what had been hit.

The first thing I noticed was the buried TV cable between our house and the street wasn't buried anymore. About half of it was out of the ground like someone had pulled it up. Most of the actual wire was vaporized, and the scorched covering was still smoldering. The lightning had struck the big, beautiful pine tree in the front yard and passed into the TV cable buried in the ground beside the big tree. A six-inch wide strip down the side of the big tree was bare where the bark had been blown off, and parts of the tree trunk were split open.

Somehow most of our electric appliances survived the lightning, but we did lose a few of them. My favorite tree, however, was completely dead in a few weeks.

I missed that big tree. That side of the yard looked so naked with it gone. So I planted a large dogwood tree and some small bushes where the pine had stood, and after a while, the new landscape started looking a little better to us. So did the rest of the neighborhood. It took about a year, but most of the tornado damage was finally repaired, and almost every house had a new roof, fresh paint, and less overgrown landscaping. Things were looking up in the old neighborhood.

Our little For the Birds business was looking good too. It was still very small, but it showed slow but consistent growth. We noticed that most people who started buying our birdseed continued to buy it. Most became loyal repeat customers. I don't know what we really expected when we started the business, but product loyalty was an exciting surprise.

Not as exciting, but much more important for our financial well-being, we were both still employed. Nancy had been at the bank for 15 years, and I had worked for five years at Four-Phase-Motorola. Five years was a new employment longevity record for me.

Although my new goal in life was to have my own business and not work for Motorola, growing a new business does take time and money. The less money you have, the more time it will take, so we still needed real jobs to survive and fund the new business. I was staying at Motorola until the new business could support me. Well, that was the plan.

"Hey Richard, the district manager wants to see you in his office." To sum up a 20-minute conversation, the district manager in the nice corner office explained that Motorola, having absorbed Four-Phase, was now merging divisions and cutting costs. Also, the newer Motorola computer technology would be replacing the older systems our division serviced. The bottom line, most of the technical support staff were no longer needed, and lucky me, I was included in the first round to be terminated.

I was a little stunned by the news, although there had been rumors going around for a few months. I just didn't think it would happen that soon or that it would happen to me. But, for some reason, being terminated did not bother me as much as it should have.

As I listened to the details of my termination, my mind was racing ahead, calculating my next move. Dust off and update the old resume, call some employment recruiters, cut expenses, and tell Nancy; oh boy, that would be the worst part. We had been doing so well, and I had to tell her I was unemployed again.

Then the manager said something that brought my wandering mind back to the conversation. "Excuse me, what did you say?" He repeated, "Your generous severance package will be sent to you within a week. You need to take all your personal items with you today, and you must return the company car within one week. That should give you enough time to purchase another car".

I immediately recognized a major problem with his plan for my future. Purchase another car? "Could you please tell me where an unemployed man can buy a car?" I sarcastically asked. There was a somewhat long, awkward silence at that point. Neither of us had an answer to that question.

The district manager was a nice guy stuck with a really bad task, and he had a lot of those meetings to get through. I told him I was fine and would have the company car back on time.

As I gathered my things, I told Dan what had happened. He was a fellow tech, a good friend, and he was shocked by the news. He saw the proverbial writing on the wall for himself.

When I mentioned that the worst part was losing my company car, Dan didn't hesitate and offered me the use of an old VW he had.

"Oh, hi Nancy, yes, I did get home a little early today. How was my day? Well, not too bad. I lost my job, and they're taking my company car, but that's ok because Dan is letting me borrow his old Volkswagen if it still runs."

I was 43 years old and unemployed again. At least this time, I didn't contribute to my own fate; it was totally out of my hands, small consolation, but it helped me deal with the situation. I knew the routine all too well, update my resume, and start making calls.

I could not help but think about our little business. It wasn't near big enough to provide income, and even worse, it would probably be the first casualty of the upcoming financial hardships that seemed inevitable. All the uncountable hours of work we had put into our new enterprise would be wasted, and my best chance of fulfilling a dream would vaporize.

I got right to work, and within a few days, I updated my resume, got a stack printed, and even mailed out a few in response to help-wanted ads. And the good news, Dan's old VW did run, and that gave me a way to get around. I was ready for another job-hunting challenge. Then I got a phone call.

The manager of Motorola's computer services southeast region, the manager who terminated me, had a problem. The head of Motorola's southeast sales division also had a problem. The person who ran the Sales Division's data center was retiring in a month, and they still had not found a qualified replacement. The head of the sales division had called the head of the computer service division because the sales division used Four-Phase computers, and I had been the systems engineer solving their computer system problems for the past two years. They really, really wanted to talk with me.

The computer service division's problem was they had just terminated me. That is why I received a very cordial phone call from the guy who terminated me. He wanted to know if I had found another position yet, and if not, would I perhaps be interested in meeting with the sales division to discuss their impending job opening. And, "Oh, could you be over there tomorrow morning, please?".

Thanks to Dan's trusty old VW, I made it to the interview and discreetly parked at the far end of the parking lot, so that I wouldn't be seen in that clunker Volkswagen. I was getting good at doing that.

The "interview" was more like a coming home party. I knew the facility; I had spent a lot of time with the retiring data center manager and even met a few upper managers. Basically, they liked me, and I liked them, so I left with them telling me they would talk it over and get back to me the next day. They called me early the next day and made me a good offer. It was more than I had been making, but I still whined a little about the 35-mile commute, each way in traffic, and the loss of my company car. They upped the offer, and I said, "Thank you very much.".

Since I was on a winning streak, I asked if I could wait two weeks to start because I was suffering from corporate-induced unemployment and emotional whiplash, and needed a little time to catch my breath. They said no because there were only three weeks left to work with the current manager before he left.

They only had one more "no" for me. I could not keep the nice severance package I had received when I was terminated. At least, I asked. I understood because, technically, my termination was canceled, and I was given a promotion and a nice raise. I was hoping they would overlook that severance package deal.

I was employed once again, with a nice raise, so Nancy and I decided to give back Dan's old VW and buy a new vehicle for me. Dan's old Volkswagen was a lifesaver, but I was not going to miss it.

We decided to get a small, no-frills Toyota pickup truck. They were dependable, got great gas mileage, and it could haul birdseed. We added a camper top over the bed to keep the seed dry. That little truck felt like our first company vehicle, and that made us feel like the little company was a real business and not just a hobby.

Things settled down again. I was still employed, making a little more money, and our little home-based enterprise continued to grow. We had even convinced a few local retail stores to carry the For the Birds brand of birdseed, and our local catalog sales were still growing. Nancy and I had less and less free time, but we ended the year with about $10,000 in catalog sales and $20,000 in wholesale seed sales.

While that was good money for a part-time, garage-based business in the 1980s, our sales volume wasn't enough to get us better discounts on our bulk seed purchases. But we were making a small profit. Every bit of that profit, and any extra money we could save, was used to cover the expanding inventory we needed. The good news, we were not losing money, and the business was growing.

Betting it All

In early 1988, I realized that our little hobby-turned-business could grow much larger. We kept gaining new customers and losing very few. Our customer retention rate was very high even though it wasn't easy to do business with us. Customers had to mail us an order form and a check for payment. Many of the customers who lived close by liked to leave an order on our answering machine, and we would deliver. They would not get their order until we could deliver on the weekends. Yet, even with all the obstacles, customers kept buying.

The customers really seemed to appreciate that we could, and would, actually answer their wild bird questions and help them make informed choices about birdseed and bird feeders. They could not get that type of help anywhere else.

The path we had started down several years earlier was looking more and more like it could lead to our dream of owning our own business, one that could support both of us. In the meantime, working was all we were doing. With very long commutes, our full-time jobs filled up the weekdays; mixing and bagging the birdseed was normal for some of the weeknights, and order deliveries and paperwork capped off the weekends. That was our life, and we were fine with that because we felt like we were winning the game.

It was becoming clear that the little For the Birds business was as large as it could ever be as a part-time, local delivery birdseed service; for our business to really grow beyond that point, our products and services needed to be visible and available to more people. We needed a retail location. We needed a store.

For the next few months, I had continuous debates between "me" and "myself" about what to do. "Me" was touting the benefits of opening a retail store. Open a store; the people will come, and we will be working for ourselves and making a lot of money. Then "myself" would bring up some minor points for discussion, like I didn't know anything about owning or operating a retail store or any other business. It was also highly unlikely I had or could get enough money to open a store. And, to make the decision even more frightening, I had read that the odds were heavily against a small, new concept retail store being successful. One of those spontaneous moments of stunning mental clarity would have come in handy at that point, but I had to work those decisions out by myself.

Nancy and I never really sat down and made a firm decision. It was more like the old slippery slope analogy where we eased onto the slope, and the further we went, the less chance we had of turning back. We had decided by default.

The next few months were spent refining the store's concept and learning everything I could about starting a small business, a real one. I felt the biggest hurdle would be securing financing, probably from a bank that made small business loans guaranteed by the Small Business Administration. I would also have to find a suitable retail location with affordable rent. Investigating retail spaces was first because I needed to know the cost before working on a loan.

I admit the first few commercial properties I investigated gave me a harsh reality check. I had no idea rents for retail locations were that high. Of course, I had experience renting apartments and was familiar with the typical yearly apartment leases and their cost. But even knowing how expensive apartments were, nothing prepared me for the cost of decent retail space.

The rental rates were very high. Then they added what is called "CAM," short for care and maintenance charges, to the base rate. CAM is your space's pro-rata share of the cost for the complex's insurance, trash disposal, landscape upkeep, general building maintenance, property and liability insurance, city and county property taxes, and several other miscellaneous costs. Also, the minimum lease term was three years. It appeared that securing a good retail space would create a significantly larger liability than I thought it would.

My next step was to create a business plan. Being a management major, this was something I knew how to do. The business plan, to me, was like a resume and needed to look professional to make a good impression. I created a plan showing the worst-case sales projections, the best case, and the average. In reality, the sales figures were a reasonable guess since I had no similar stores to compare mine with. I used the average sales of several specialty retail stores in the area and plugged those numbers into my projections. I attached a few neighborhood newspaper articles that had been written about our little "cottage industry" and some national articles about the growth of the bird-watching hobby. We were looking good on paper.

In addition to the business plan, Nancy and I created a personal plan. We needed a plan because opening a store was very different than working out of the house. Someone would have to be there all the time, which meant they would have to quit their real job. Nancy was the logical choice to quit her job and run the store since I was earning more money and she would be better at working with the customers. Besides, after 16 years, Nancy was past ready to leave the bank.

Our plan was simple and direct. Nancy would quit her good job at the bank; we would take on massive debt and open a small retail store with a 50% chance of success, at best. What could possibly go wrong? Well, we actually considered the possibility that it could all go very wrong. If it did, we would be bankrupt and maybe homeless. I would still have a job, but we would have to start at the bottom and rebuild our life. Certainly not a pleasant thought, but a real possibility that had to be faced.

Nancy and I did have several honest discussions about that worst-case scenario and decided that this was our best chance to catch a dream. I felt that failing would be better than not trying, always wondering if we would have succeeded, and always regretting that we didn't try.

We had a business plan. We had a personal plan. We narrowed the store location down to two spaces. We had a floor plan for each location, and we knew what products, other than our birdseed, we would stock. We had even decided on a business name, the Bird Watcher Supply Company, which we promptly registered.

For the Birds was kept as a brand name for our birdseed line. By then, all we needed was money. I called a local bank that issued SBA loans and scheduled an appointment to speak with the loan manager.

Just before the big meeting, we sat in the car and rehearsed our sales pitch. We were ready. The meeting went well through the hellos and handshakes, and the banker was very impressed with our business plan. Then he asked in a slow-metered voice, "So you want to open a store that only sells birdseed?" We replied with a verbal list of other items, like bird feeders, houses, birdbaths, books, and wild bird-related gift items. He did not get it from the look on his face, but I don't think that mattered. It would be an SBA-guaranteed loan which would greatly reduce the risk to the bank. It was looking good.

I think he made a mental assessment that we knew what we were doing, whatever it was, and we were dressed nicely. "Well, everything here looks good, so how much money do you need?" We told him, and he tilted his head as a furrowed brow appeared on his face. We knew something was wrong. There were a thousand things he could have said at that point that we could have understood, but "I'm sorry, you don't need enough money." was not one of them. I did not have a quick comeback for that. The best I could come up with was "what?" The furrowed brow had shifted to my face.

The banker explained that SBA loans had minimum and maximum limits, and our needs were below the minimum. Below the minimum? I was stunned. It seemed like an awful lot of money to me. We were sitting in a bank applying for a loan, and the man was telling us we did not need enough money to qualify for a loan. After I gained my composure, I suggested I go out to the car, change the business plan to show we needed more money, come back in and start over. Loan managers don't seem to have a well-developed sense of humor.

After recovering for a few days, we went to bank number two. It was a smaller independent bank, and the bank president took us into his office to listen to our pitch. He was very complimentary of our business plan and said too many people came in with just some notes. He actually said it was the best plan he had seen. We were off to a good start. Another advantage of this banker was that he enjoyed feeding wild birds, so he knew what we were talking about. Since he was not pushing for an SBA loan, he was more cautious about our ability to succeed and pay back the loan.

After a good half hour of talking, the banker was still hesitant to commit, so Nancy kept talking about us and our cottage business and how it would do in a real store. She wore him down, and he made us an offer. The loan was for a little less than we were asking for, but he would do it if we thought we could get started for that amount. I felt that we could cut back on initial inventory and pay Nancy a little less. We had a deal! We left some of our For the Birds birdseed with him as a thank you. That was the beginning of a very long financial and personal relationship.

With money to buy inventory, some store fixtures, and a big lighted sign for the storefront, we were ready to decide on a store location. We chose a new strip center across from a major mall. There was good visibility and a lot of street traffic. Even better, the landlord was anxious to fill the center and willing to take a chance on a new business. He helped us with the "build-out" items like an office space with a view of the sales floor, a sales counter, and a simulated wood deck with railings to highlight our birdseed and display bird feeders. Of course, he built those costs into the rent payments, those huge monthly rent payments. The total cost of the three-year lease was far more than our house had cost. All we had to do was sign the lease and pay two months' rent upfront.

That sounded easier to do than it was. The lease documents were in front of us, the pens, compliments of the landlord, were in our hands, and there were big numbers all over those papers. Nancy and I were extremely nervous and what-ifs ran rampant in my head. What if no one likes our store? What if we aren't good at running a retail store? What if we lose our house and everything? Then a "what if" popped up that got my new pen moving across that paper; what if we don't try?

Once that contract was signed, we were the proud owners of our first store, or more correctly, a plain, empty, very expensive retail space and a dream.

The landlord saw how nervous we were, smiled, and told us he would be nervous about working with us if we weren't nervous about making such a big commitment. However, he added that he felt we had a good chance of making it work. We hoped he was right.

The bank and the landlord now owned everything we had. In gambling terms, we had gone "all in."

We timed everything to open a little before Christmas, which gave the landlord's construction crew and us almost two months to finish the space and time for us to put in all the store fixtures, display the products, and get ready for opening day. Even though the contractor had some delays because of building code inspections, the crew finished the office area, stockroom wall, sales counter, and the simulated porch deck on schedule. The flooring and painting were completed just in time for Nancy to set up the merchandise and hire some help.

Nancy had resigned from her position at the bank and was officially our first employee. She was also officially making half as much as she did at that bank. But she jumped in and started handling all the details of stocking and decorating the store. She hired an assailant and the two of them, with my part-time help, had everything ready to go by opening day.

Just to be clear, our store was in no way comparable to the slick, national chain stores you see in malls. Our store was a little rustic, and you could even say somewhat plain. One of the display tables in the store was taken from our house. We also took our television, stereo, and speakers to the store so we could play the nature-themed videotapes and nature sound music CDs we had for sale. We were not going to have time for watching television and listening to music at home anyway.

We had placed a few small ads in local papers, but we had no idea what to expect. The old saying from the Field of Dreams movie, "Build it, and they will come," sounds wonderful, but what if they don't come? The hour before we opened was a period of emotional extremes. We had done it. We owned a specialty retail store, the Bird Watcher Supply store in Kennesaw, Georgia. We were proud and excited. Yet, at the same time, I had a gut-wrenching fear that I had made the biggest mistakes of my life.

Opening Day

A few minutes after we opened the doors, a customer walked in, and it was not a neighbor, a well-wishing friend, or a current catalog customer. Instead, the person had seen the sign go up a few weeks earlier and wanted to drop by to see what we had. Another customer popped in, and they had seen one of our ads. But, again, we did not know them, which was very encouraging.

As we started working with the customers, our nervousness settled down, and we found it easy to answer their questions and help them. I was surprised at how well each customer interaction went. I should not have been so nervous because we had already spent three years talking to people about attracting more birds with better birdseed, which bird feeders worked the best, and how to stop the squirrels from eating the birdseed. We actually knew what we were talking about, and the customers responded to our recommendations.

We were not overrun with shoppers that first day, but business was steady. When the doors closed that evening and we looked at the cash register sales figures, we had done more business than I thought we would. We were relieved and happy but still a little worried about what would happen after day one?

We got better at working with customers as the days went by, and operating the cash register and restocking shelves became easier. Since we were open seven days a week, Nancy worked every day in the store, and I dropped by after work to help where I could. We both were there on the weekends.

December went by quickly, and we had a really good month with more Christmas gift shopping for birdseed and feeders, our core products, than I had expected. It was a good start, and we were excited about the coming year.

A few months into the new year, our sales were even higher. We used all the extra money for more inventory to replace what had sold and to make the store look full. The good cash flow allowed us to place larger inventory orders which saved on shipping and earned larger discounts.

Halfway into our first full year, we knew we needed to expand. The little 1,200-square-foot store was just too small. The space beside us in the strip center was still vacant, so we took it. That addition doubled the store's size. We also took that opportunity to make the store look a little more professional. We added a few new merchandise displays and built a garden area with a stone pathway and a little wooden fence around it. It made a great display area decorated with artificial plants and filled with birdbaths, statuary, and garden accent merchandise.

With the additional space and a total store renovation, we looked more like a professional retail store. It was about that time I realized that all the various jobs I held before we opened the store had prepared me well for the wide variety of challenges and problems inherent in small specialty retailing. If something broke, I could fix it. I could build displays, handle electrical problems, paint walls, organize a stockroom, program the cash registers, manage the business finances, and handle most of the other things a small business requires.

None of those skills were particularly noteworthy on their own, but together, they were invaluable to me as I worked with the little birdseed operation and the new retail store.

I had another reason to think we would succeed; I had Nancy. Once she was out of the bank and in the store, she quickly demonstrated she could operate a retail store and do it well. It was also apparent she was pretty good at managing me. I happen to be a somewhat compulsive and always impatient risk-taker with a poor sense of other people's character. Nancy, however, is a steady, cautious, very detail-oriented person who has a sharp memory and a keen perception of people. Not only was she an essential asset to our business, but she was a much-needed balance to my particular personality traits. We made a great team, which was becoming more important as the pace of our businesses picked up.

The sales at the store were still better than we had hoped and still growing. At that same time, our little wholesale seed business was growing, and we could not keep up by bagging seed at night in our garage. The seed business had become more than we could handle and too big for the garage.

I managed to find a small, usable space at a local feed and seed store where we bought our corn. It wasn't fancy, but it was available, bigger than our garage and really cheap. I ran an ad for part-time help and quickly got some local college students who liked the idea of being able to work around their school schedules. Our seed production was soon back on track.

That year turned out to be very hectic. A lot of things were changing, and not just with the business. All of a sudden, the kids were not kids anymore.

Elaine graduated from college with a high-grade point average and a degree in psychology, but it had not been an easy road for her. In addition to the everyday problems and pressures of attending college, Elaine had to change schools in the middle of her studies to find lower tuition costs.

Elaine was also having a hard time dealing with her mother's new husband, but through it all, she held it together and earned her degree. Elaine had started showing the personal attributes it takes to do well in life.

Michael was showing promise also. He had stuck with the Boy Scouts program as he grew up and always worked hard to move up through the ranks. That year, Michael became an Eagle Scout, scouting's highest rank. That accomplishment at that age told me a lot about Michael. It let me know he also had the ability and drive to do well in life, and I was a very proud Dad. I began to realize I had two really great kids.

After Elaine graduated, she began searching for work. The job market was a little tight, and entry-level jobs were hard to find. When I heard about an administrative assistant position at Motorola, I arranged for Elaine to come in for an interview, and she did the rest. Elaine was hired, and her first assignment was to organize the central file storage room.

All the paperwork for the Radio Communications Division's contracts was stored there, and the sales staff and admin help had done a great job of putting anything and everything anywhere and everywhere. I think this was a test for the new girl. "Let's put her in the 'room of doom' and see what happens. I bet she doesn't last a week."

The room of doom had met its match. She quickly had it cleaned up and totally organized. But, in her sweet southern way, she also let everyone know they had better not mess up her room. Being impressed, the VP took her out of that file room and made her his assistant for all his special projects. After Elaine made it clear that she didn't type and didn't fetch coffee, they seemed to get along quite nicely. Everyone soon knew Elaine, the VP's new, young, good-looking assistant who just happened to be talented.

However, very few people in the building besides the department heads and a few others actually knew much about me. They did know I had a cubicle on the top floor across the aisle from the offices of the comptroller, the accounting manager, and the regional vice president. They also knew I had access to every "No One Allowed" and "Do Not Enter" room in the building, and I was often seen in the high-level meetings and going in and out of the department managers' offices.

Actually, I did have a pretty cool job. I handled all computer software and hardware acquisitions, support and data security issues, and any data and phone communications software or hardware problems. I even got to design and manage the construction of a special room for a new high-tech phone system. It was "Authorized Personnel Only," of course.

Basically, if it plugged in and had a problem, it was my problem. I did not interface with many people, so few in the building knew what I really did. I suppose my job made me look somewhat mysterious and important, but I was really just a high-tech maintenance man keeping the data and communications systems humming.

However, some of the more observant employees did manage to notice I had a wedding band, and I wasn't spending all my time in secret rooms because they had seen me, more than once, in the break area having lunch with the VP's new special assistant. Even more gossip-worthy, the young lady and I had been seen going out to "lunch" together often.

It had to happen; Elaine and I were spotted leaving work together in my car one evening. Oh yes, we had become an "item," the hottest topic sweeping through the maze of office cubicles. The rampant rumors spread quickly. The news of our sordid and illicit affair had gone viral among the company's gossip junkies. Finally, one brave lady, whose curiosity was killing her, summoned up the nerve to ask Elaine about her "relationship" with Richard, the mystery man.

I'm sure the gossip lady was expecting Elaine to deny even knowing me or spill out all the juicy details of the affair. "Oh, Richard is my dad," Elaine replied. POP! That unexpected answer burst the rumor balloon and deflated the rampant speculation that had been building for weeks. I have often thought, that if Elaine and I had known what they were thinking, we really could have had some serious fun with those people.

Later that year, Elaine joined the family business. Since I was still at Motorola and Nancy was running our store, we needed someone to take over the For the Birds seed packaging operation. Elaine was suddenly responsible for supervising the part-time workers who packaged the seed products, ordering the bulk seed ingredients, and making all local deliveries to our wholesale customers. So, she got to maintain and drive our "new" delivery truck; a very old bread delivery step van. It was, "Here, Elaine, take over." She didn't know it at the time, but she had just started a career.

Bringing Elaine on board to handle the seed business was a crucial move at the right time because things were changing fast for our little enterprise. The store was doing great, and that did not escape the attention of our landlord, who dropped by with an offer we couldn't refuse. He had another strip center about 15 miles away, and he really, really wanted us to put a Bird Watcher Supply store there. He said we were doing so well we needed to expand to other locations. Then, of course, he would say that because we would then write him two large monthly rent checks. But actually, he was a great guy, had our best interests in mind, and believed in our concept and ability to succeed. I was already thinking about another store, but that would be a very risky decision. I would need to run the new store and that would require quitting my job at Motorola, the job that was paying the bills.

Our first store was making a profit, but it was all going to pay off the startup loan, fund the expansion and bring in more inventory. A quick calculation pointed out that I, like Nancy, would have to pay myself a lot less money than I was making at Motorola. A new store would have to turn profitable quickly, or we would quickly be in a major financial bind.

Nancy and I talked about it, analyzed it, and then ignored all the scary stuff and a fair amount of logic and decided to go for it. We started planning for Bird Watcher Supply Company number two, and one of the considerations was when I would leave Motorola. We decided it should be February or March, only about four months away. I wasn't sure if I was smart or an idiot; sometimes, there isn't much difference.

About a month later, my boss, the accounting manager, asked me to come with him to a meeting in the division VP's office. My boss did not look happy, and no meeting with an unhappy boss had worked out well for me in the past. As we walked into the meeting, my mind was racing. "How could they fire me? I hadn't done anything wrong. I thought they all liked me and the job I was doing." I knew I was going to resign in a few months anyway, but I wanted to go out on my terms as a matter of pride.

The meeting was small, just the vice president, the comptroller, the department managers, and me. I was not a department manager, but I was responsible for the technology systems. The others in the room managed people and I managed the things they used, so I was invited to the party. The meeting was brief, to the point, and somber. The southeast regional headquarters for radio communications was shutting down. The process would be staged over months.

The official announcement and all the details were to be presented at a meeting of all employees the next week. The VP wanted us to submit lists of functions we could do without during the shutdown process and those we needed until the end. That was it. We scheduled a few meetings to coordinate our lists and went back to our offices. Well, technically speaking, I wasn't being fired, just permanently laid off.

The big meeting with all employees shocked most of them, even though rumors had been circulating for a while. A personnel officer from the company headquarters conducted the meeting. After a brief explanation of what was happening and why, he announced some employees would be terminated, released as he phrased it, in thirty days and others between then and the final closing date. Essential personnel, like myself, would be the last to go.

The speaker also highlighted the generous severance packages everyone would receive if they stayed until their scheduled termination date. When the meeting ended, most people stayed around, some alone, some huddled in small groups, and some crying. They were just trying to assimilate what had just happened to their lives.

That was a very traumatic event for most of the employees, and I felt really bad for them, but for a change losing my job had worked out well for me. During my last few months, I used my remaining vacation time to handle a lot of the preparations for opening store number two in Roswell, Georgia, another Atlanta suburb. The nice severance package would really help as I transitioned from the corporate world to living as a retail business owner.

A Rare Christmas Present

We opened the Roswell store in March of 1990, and I don't know if I was more excited about opening that store or because I was finally working for myself. Nancy and I were both officially self-employed. Recognizing this accomplishment helped a little to overcome the sheer terror of not having real jobs.

As we settled into our new routines, it didn't take us long to realize that operating two stores meant twice the work. We had more employees to manage and even more paperwork. The second store also meant more merchandise to order and receive and more checks to write. Then there were the utilities, rents, insurance, advertising, and the list went on.

Nancy and I had saved money by doing the payroll, paying the bills, and keeping the books ourselves. But with two stores, we no longer had the time. We reluctantly hired an accountant to handle those functions. It started to feel like we were working just to pay all those other people, but we were also paying down the startup loans; that realization alone was quite uplifting and motivating.

As the new store headed into its first Christmas season, its sales had been as expected, good but not great. Then, the store received a rare present that resulted in a dramatic increase in new customers and sales.

It was closing time on Christmas Eve when Sally went out the back of the store to empty the trash and fill the bird feeders we kept there in the alleyway. She was only outside briefly before she rushed back in and, almost shouting, exclaimed, "There's a hummingbird at the feeder in the back! I just saw a hummingbird!". I grabbed the binoculars and eased out the back door, hoping to get a look at what Sally had seen. It was late afternoon and overcast, so when I did see the bird, I could tell it was a hummingbird but could not see enough detail to identify the species. I waited another half an hour, but it did not return; it was past its bedtime.

I know this doesn't sound like something worth being excited about, as it was just a hummingbird at a hummingbird feeder. But this was late December, and according to the conventional wisdom at the time, all the hummingbirds in North America should have migrated south to Central America a few months earlier.

The exceptions were a few birds of several species that would spend the winters along parts of the warm coastline areas of the Gulf of Mexico and California. There were occasional reports of hummingbirds being seen inland in winter, but those birds were thought to be too ill or too stupid to migrate south, and they would definitely perish in the winter cold.

So why did I have a hummingbird feeder hanging outside in the winter if the hummers were not supposed to be here? I had heard about a man in neighboring Alabama who had a particular love of hummingbirds and was conducting research on migrating birds. That man and his equally dedicated wife had a particular curiosity about the occasional reports of hummingbirds being spotted in wintertime in northern Alabama, the hummingbirds that were not supposed to be there and would surely die.

I heard he was looking for leads to find more of those winter hummingbirds, and one or two of my store customers had mentioned they were still seeing a hummingbird come to their feeder in late November. I contacted the hummingbird expert and passed along the information; that's how I met Bob and Martha Sargent.

Bob came over to Georgia and captured, documented, and released the very healthy hummingbird. It was a Rufous hummingbird, a western species not supposed to be found in the eastern United States in any season.

I had kept a hummingbird feeder outside that winter because I knew if someone else could have one of those rare visitors, maybe I could too.

By sunrise Christmas morning, Nancy and I were set up in the alley behind the store, our camera on a tripod and binoculars in our hands, waiting to see if that little bird was still around and still alive.

It wasn't long before we spotted the bird back at the feeder. It appeared to be a young male Ruby-throat because it was green with a small group of dark feathers on the front of its white throat.

That bird certainly appeared healthy as it returned to feed about every forty-five minutes. We stayed there for five or six hours, observing the bird and taking pictures. To be sure it was a Ruby-throat, I wanted to see the few dark feathers on the throat catch sunlight and reflect their ruby red color. But with every glimpse of the bird, I only saw black. I blamed it on the overcast sky.

We finished up Christmas Day at home, going through hummingbird identification books. I had narrowed the possibilities down to either a young male Ruby-throated, a high probability, or a Black-chinned hummingbird, which would be a long shot at best. Black-chinned hummingbirds reside in the far western United States and had never been recorded as far east as Georgia.

A few days after Christmas, I was finally able to get my film developed, and sometimes, nothing is something. I had good photographs taken from various angles and still could see no trace of red reflecting from those few little feathers high on the throat area. If that bird had been a Ruby-throated, some red should have been visible.

I felt confident the bird was a young male Black-chinned Hummingbird. If true, that would be a first for Georgia and a very big deal. My conclusion was a guess, but I felt it was a really good one. It was time to call the expert.

Bob was very excited to hear what I thought the bird was, excited but cautious. A week later, Bob made the trip from Alabama to Roswell, Georgia. There were just a few people there because we wanted to be sure about that bird before announcing the rare find.

It was one exciting moment when Bob had the bird in his hand and saw the black feathers on the upper throat and the final proof, a few small purple feathers on the lower throat area, which had just emerged in the last few days. Male Black-chinned humming-birds have a narrow band of feathers on the lower throat that reflect purple.

The bird was measured, weighed, photographed, and had a tiny, numbered identification band placed on its leg. It was given a drink of sugar water from a small feeder, then taken outside and released. It was official; the bird was a juvenile Black-chinned hummingbird and the first-ever recorded in Georgia.

Georgia's first documented Black-chinned Hummingbird

Word spread quickly, and a lot of people wanted to see that bird. A local TV station even came to the store to film the bird and interview people. The station created a nice little story about the rare bird, and it got several plays on prime-time news in the Atlanta area.

Many serious birdwatchers, along with other curious people, came to see the bird. Everyone would park in front, walk through the store, and out the back door, where they could stand behind a camouflage screen and watch the bird come to the feeder across the alley. Many of the visitors actually shopped in the store until someone announced the bird was at the feeder. Sales were really good.

That bird stayed for two more weeks before moving on. So many people got to see a bird newly discovered in Georgia. I got credit for finding it, and the store got a lot of free publicity. That little bird turned out to be one very special Christmas present.

Nancy putting fresh nectar out for the Black-chinned Hummingbird.

Over the next few months, I received a few more calls from people who had seen the story on TV and wanted to report seeing a hummingbird in their yard. People were listening to our message that they should leave a hummingbird feeder out during the winter and report any hummer they saw from November through February. Every few weeks, I would get a report from the metro Atlanta area and pass it to Bob, who would investigate the sighting. Most of the birds we documented were the Rufous species, but we occasionally found a new species in the state.

Martha Sargent has been very generous with thanks for all the assistance we provided initially and through the years. We made a great team. I, through my stores, got people to look for and report hummingbirds during the winter. With their dedication and hard work, Bob and Martha were able to document the presence of so many new hummingbird species in the southeastern states.

In the early 1990s, the Ruby-throated was the only hummingbird species documented in Georgia. Since then, 12 new species have been added to Georgia's list.

Bob is no longer with us, but his work goes on through a few dedicated people Bob trained to carry on the research.

By 1992, Nancy and I had both stores under control, or stated more accurately, we had adjusted to running two stores. Even though finances were always very tight, we were not as concerned that we could go out of business any day as we were in the first year or two. It was very long and tiring work, but we were doing it and very happy about how it was going.

Part of the fun was meeting all the customers, helping them, and learning from them. Another great thing about the stores was the other opportunities it brought our way, like participating in hummingbird research. One of those opportunities came when I answered the phone at the Roswell store one day.

The man on the phone asked for Mr. Cole, and I answered, "That's me; what can I help you with today?" The man explained that he was with the Georgia Department of Natural Resources and would like me to come to the "DNR" main office in downtown Atlanta for a meeting.

I don't know why, but I get the "what have I done this time" feeling every time I hear something like that. He explained that the department was looking for someone for a special project, and somebody recommended me. He did not want to go into much detail on the phone. But hearing that somebody had recommended me for something stirred my curiosity.

I had to admit it was a very interesting meeting. The State Parks and Historic Sites Division of the DNR had two problems they needed to fix.

One, the hotels and visitor centers in the state's parks contained gift shops, but the operation of those shops was at the very bottom of the park's to-do list. Park managers did not want to use scarce park personnel to operate the gift shops. So, the shops were not staffed well; there was no inventory control, in or out, and no one could tell if they were making or losing money, since the gift shops' expenses and receipts were thrown in with the hotels' or visitor center's totals.

Problem number two was that the profits, if there were any, went into the state's general fund. When it was time for the state to dole out those funds to all departments in the state, the parks always seemed to be left groveling for the leftovers.

Some smart people at the DNR had come up with a plan to solve the problems and were ready to test it. They would pick one of the state's gift shops, sell its operation to a non-profit origination for a dollar, and have the non-profit operate the store like a real, private business, then donate all profits back to the parks department. Doing that would free up state parks personnel for important park work and possibly bring some much-needed revenue back to the parks.

All they needed to do was find someone good at operating small retail stores and convince them to run the gift shops as a volunteer.

I can just picture the officials in that room breaking out in stomach-cramping laughter, slapping their hands on the table, and hollering. "Oh, that's a good one! Give them a store, have them run it for free, and give us all the profits! Oh, my side hurts! Man, that's hilarious!". Then someone said, "Hey, wait a minute, there is this one guy I know, and I think we should call him."

My state government needed my help; how could I say no? Over the next few months, the plan was implemented with the state's approval. I created a 503-C non-profit with the chosen name, North Georgia Heritage Association. That corporation joined the Bird Watcher Supply Co. and For the Birds in my collection of corporate paperwork residing on a table in my spare bedroom.

We acquired the first gift shop in a state-run hotel just 65 miles north of my house. The short commute helped a lot.

I had the full corporation of the state park's officials, the park's manager, and staff. I was also assigned a liaison staffer at DNR headquarters to help me bridge the gap between government bureaucracy and my sometimes direct and impatient approach to solving a problem. A board of directors was gathered, and I was named chairman. We were ready to go.

The gift shop had three main problems. One, slow-selling items just sat on shelves taking up valuable space, and great sellers were quickly sold and not replaced. Two, far too often, there was no one in the gift shop to ring up a sale or help a customer, which created problem number three. Far too many items were just disappearing.

Everyone got busy. The state park ran a local help wanted ad, and I showed up for the interviews. We hired a full-time manager and a part-time helper. We brought in more appropriate merchandise, displayed it properly, and had a real store employee help the customers. We also made inventory management a top priority. Within a few months, the little gift shop was making money.

During the next two years, North Georgia Heritage was able to attract some quality members to serve on the Association's board of directors, and our little success at the first park led to other parks wanting us to help them. The additional park gift shops to manage, plus working with my board of directors and state personnel, started taking more of my time just as Bird Watcher Supply and For the Birds needed more attention.

After two years, I submitted my resignation as chairman. I was asked to stay as vice-chairman, mostly in an advisory role, and I accepted. That allowed me to stay involved, although to a much less degree, and contribute to that unique public/private venture's success. I remained in the vice president/advisor capacity for six years.

Over those years we acquired state park stores in other parts of the state and the organization's name was changed to the Georgia Heritage Association to include the whole state. I feel good about being a part of that organization's formation and growth. Today it is known as the Friends of Georgia State Parks and Historic Sites, and its main mission is to act as an umbrella group fostering and helping the many local friends of parks associations.

Our help with the Georgia DNR led us to yet another opportunity to help with a problem in our state. You do not hear much about it today, but by the 1960s and 1970s, the Bald Eagles were in a serious population decline.

In her famous 1962 book "Silent Spring," Rachael Carson pointed the finger at the decades-long and widespread use of agricultural chemical pesticides like DDT. That book helped heighten awareness about the impact of chemicals on the environment and also the loss of suitable habitats for the birds. Those concerns motivated activists and built public support for change. Within ten years, conservation laws had been strengthened, and DDT was banned in the United States.

Unfortunately, the Bald Eagle population had reached a low of only 417 breeding pairs in the entire lower 48 states by then. The Bald Eagles were struggling to repopulate and had become an endangered species.

Georgia only found a single nesting pair of eagles in a 1978 search. Like other states that had lost eagle populations, Georgia became more aggressive in its attempts to restore eagle populations to a sustainable level. Georgia began participation in relocation programs where young birds were obtained from captive breeding facilities and wild nests in states where the birds were more numerous. This program was not cheap, so the state was always looking for means to acquire extra funds to bring in more birds to be released in Georgia.

When the DNR asked me to help raise money for the project, Nancy and I were happy to help because this was directly helping wild birds. We put five-gallon water jugs with nice "Adopt an Eagle" signs on our Bird Watcher stores' sales counters. We also pushed the fundraising effort in our newsletters and advertising. Our customers were generous and happy to contribute to such a great cause. And we raised enough money to "adopt" the first eagle in a few months.

The process of relocating nestling eagles takes coordination and timing. The eagles brought into Georgia came from the northwestern states. Each donor nest needed to be monitored to determine that at least two baby eagles were present and healthy. A schedule of when to remove one of the young birds would be set depending on the projected date the young birds would leave the nest. A bird would be relocated well before the date it should leave its nest, but late enough for the bird to do well without its parents.

It takes about three months for baby eagles to develop to the point they can leave the nest. When their time came, the eagles were removed from their nests, taken to an airport, and flown to Atlanta. The birds were then transported to a remote release site on a large lake north of Atlanta.

Once at the lake, one of the rangers and I placed the young eagles in a release tower, where they would stay until ready to fly. The release tower

was like a large enclosed treehouse mounted high on four tall telephone poles. The front and part of the sides of the large holding area were covered with vertical bars to give the eagles a penthouse view of the lake while preventing them from leaving too early. A pile of large sticks placed on the cage floor simulated a real

nest. There was a platform on the back of the cage area where a volunteer could stand, without being seen, and drop food through a large tube into the cage.

The volunteer would climb the tower every few days and provide the growing birds with tasty roadkill animals and freshly caught fish. Then, when the birds showed signs they were ready to fly, the bars on the front of the little room would be opened, and the birds would be free to leave when they were ready.

We were able to help fund the relocation of five eagles over several years, and the highlight for me was getting to place two of those, not-so-small, baby eagles into their release tower.

That program was a great example of federal and state governments, local level donors, and a lot of volunteers coming together to achieve a worthy goal. That program was a tremendous success, and by 2007, the Bald Eagle was removed from the Endangered Species List. Today these majestic birds are widespread and growing in numbers.

Because we were already involved with the Georgia DNR on several programs, we decided it would be fun to attend their very popular

Weekend for Wildlife annual fundraising event benefitting wildlife conservation projects. The gathering at Sea Island on the Georgia coast attracts nature-loving guests from all over. They come and join DNR management and staff for a few days of lectures, presentations, special guests, and a good selection of "insider" guided visits to nearby state parks.

Nancy and I started attending those events and even donated birdseed, bird feeders, nature books, and other items for their silent auctions and raffles. One of the years we attended the event, a few of us got to go on a very special outing. We were taken to the U.S. Navy submarine base at Kings Bay, a little south of where we were. The Georgia DNR and the Kings Bay submarine base have a strong working relationship, and those of us on that visit were the beneficiaries.

The USS West Virginia, a nuclear-powered missile-launching submarine, was in port, and we were invited to come aboard. Once inside, my first thought was how cool it was to be inside a nuclear submarine. Then, as our naval officer guide showed us around, I started to grasp just how amazing that submarine was.

First, I realized the true size of that thing. Those subs look small with just part of their top out of the water, but it's almost two football fields long and houses a crew of about 150. Next, we saw the cafeteria, the crew sleeping areas, the captain's quarters, and the spaceship-like control room.

We also walked through the rows of large missile silos, 24 in all, extending from the lower part of the sub up through the floors to the outside. The huge tubes held the large Trident missiles, and each missile could carry up to eight independently controlled nuclear bomb warheads.

After a little mental math, I realized the submarine Nancy and I were walking around in could carry and accurately deliver 192 nuclear bombs. That thought, to this day, is extremely sobering.

As our tour ended, the captain autographed and handed us a nice picture of his ship. That picture still hangs in our home as a reminder of that truly unique experience.

19

All Work and
No Play

B ack at work, things were changing fast. Sales in our two retail stores increased slightly with each passing month. Our small For the Birds wholesale seed operation also attracted more Atlanta-area stores to carry our birdseed, and a lawn and garden products distributor started selling our products to a few stores in neighboring states. All of that was very encouraging, and it led us to make two major decisions in 1992.

Elaine and I decided to change the name of our birdseed business and its products. The "For the Birds" name was just a little too cute for a serious top-end birdseed brand, so we changed the company name to Cole's Wild Bird Products and created new upscale labels to highlight the high quality and family name.

Along with changing the birdseed company's name, I made Elaine the company's president and gave her a nice ownership stake; she had earned both. Of course, those things were not worth much then, but we were hoping they would be someday.

At the same time, Nancy and I decided it was time to go for store number three and we felt Duluth, Georgia, another Atlanta suburb, would be a great location. So, by the end of '92, the new Cole's brand birdseed was looking really good on the shelves of our three Bird Watcher Supply Company stores.

The new, upscale birdseed packaging also made a huge impact on our trade show exhibits. We were already producing the best birdseed products on the market and with the new packaging, we were looking like it.

Each year seemed to fly by as we worked harder and faster, but it was so exciting. We were finally carving out our little piece of the American dream.

But with all profits going to feed the expansion beast, there was never much money left for us. We still couldn't pay ourselves more than the bare minimum it took to make the payments on our little house, buy groceries, and put gas in the cars, but things were sure looking great for our growing businesses.

Our first store in Kennesaw had been expanded once before and needed to expand again. We decided, with the help of our favorite landlord, to make it much larger. It

seemed a prime space in the middle of the retail center would soon be available and he wanted us to have the first chance to grab it before it got away. I think I already mentioned that he was a good salesman. That location became one of the largest stores of its type in the country. How could we say no.

We were ten years into our little business venture and no longer felt like we could go out of business any day, and we no longer felt that the whole thing was a huge mistake.

It had been a very long and hard journey. We had worked ten or more hours a day, six and seven days a week, almost nonstop while the businesses grew, but it was an exciting period filled with many little successes and just as many tough challenges. Yet, we took comfort and encouragement in the realization we were well on our way to our dream of business success.

We should have been raising glasses of champagne and celebrating our progress, but we weren't. And, unlike the future of our two businesses, the future for us was not looking so bright. By 1997, the years of work and stress had taken a toll on both of us. Nancy and I were in full burnout mode, and our relationship was in serious trouble.

Neither of us was happy, which was very obvious in our interactions. We were mentally drained and physically exhausted all the time. We had become two emotionless robots just trudging through our required daily routines, held hostage by the two growing businesses with no end in sight and no easy way out.

It wasn't all doom and gloom; there were still some good times, but they had become fewer, and the hard, tension-filled days and nights were beginning to dominate our lives.

We didn't know what was happening at the time, but Nancy's behavior was changing. I'm sure mine was also, and I probably wasn't the easiest person to get along with either. But the normally easygoing, calm, and patient Nancy became easy to agitate, hard to please, distrustful, and suspicious of others, especially me. Nothing anyone did was good enough or done right in her mind. She was constantly stressed and had trouble sleeping.

As her symptoms worsened, she found it difficult to cope with situations like dinner at a restaurant. During one episode, we had to leave before dinner was finished because she felt panicked and just had to get out of there.

Nancy had changed; she was no longer the Nancy I knew and loved. We both were looking for answers and trying things to help her relax, but nothing worked. I even got her to take breaks each day at the office, and we would go for walks outside. That did help her for a little while after the exercise, but the anxiety always returned.

Nancy also knew something was really wrong and getting worse. She didn't understand what was happening, and she was frightened by the mental changes she was experiencing.

I don't know how close we were to calling it quits on our relationship, but I know the thoughts were in our minds, and that scared me. I kept thinking back to my breakup with Sandra, and I could see many parallels to my current situation.

It was obvious Nancy needed help and her regular doctor didn't have any good answers for her. Nancy thought there was some internal or nutritional cause behind her problems, but I began to suspect other causes and suggested we schedule a visit with a behavioral health specialist. We had nothing to lose at that point.

During the meeting with the psychologist, and after a good discussion of Nancy's medical record, current medications, and symptoms, he confidently diagnosed her with generalized anxiety disorder, and panic disorder. That diagnosis itself was a huge relief to both of us. We had a name for her problems, and the problems had specific treatments that would help her. The frightening "I don't know what's wrong with me" concerns came to an end.

The doctor suggested she begin taking some medications and strongly suggested altering the excessive time spent working.

We were working too much and for too long. It was just that simple. To paraphrase the Eagles' song, Life in the Fast Lane, "We pretended not to notice we were caught up in the race." The end result was a loss of balance in our lives, all tension and fatigue, and no rest, relaxation, or fun.

We had not knowingly pushed ourselves to that point of physical and mental collapse. We had simply pursued our dream with everything we had. We willingly made sacrifices and burned the hours to achieve our goal. If there was any fault in that pursuit, it was the ambiguous definition of success. Had we achieved our goal by opening the first store, the second? Maybe it came with the growth of our birdseed operation. Perhaps success is an elusive goal that changes its definition as you approach it.

Whether we had achieved success or not, it was no longer relevant. We had much more serious things to strive for.

Nancy's condition was much easier to diagnose than to correct. We needed to make real changes in our lives if we wanted to save our marriage and the businesses, we had worked so hard to build. We needed to spend more time on ourselves and less time working.

If we hadn't learned anything else in our years running a small business, we learned how to acknowledge and tackle problems, and this was a big one. But good timing was on our side, and after all the hard work and years of putting everything into the business, the business was finally generating more profit than we needed for our growth. So, as we rolled into 1998, we used the money to hire someone to take some of the workload off our plates.

Scott was not a wild bird expert, but he was experienced at managing people. We placed him between the stores and us. As our retail operations manager, he handled the daily operations and personnel issues at the store level. With that slice of the work pie on his plate, we had some room on our plate for a nice slice of normal life.

Nancy and I had begun the very long burnout-recovery and relationship-repair process. And, with more time to work on "us" and less time spent working on the businesses, I knew Nancy and I would be just fine.

After giving Scott time to adjust to the daily details of the Bird Watcher Supply stores, we felt everything would run fine without us being there all the time. We decided it was finally time for a real vacation, and Costa Rica looked like a great destination for bird-watching and jungle exploration. The trip would be a great way to punctuate the end of our workaholic addictions. All we needed to do was apply for some passports.

The passport application process was very simple. Show a driver's license and birth certificate, fill out some forms, and pose for your picture. It doesn't get much easier than that.

A few weeks later, the passports arrived in the mail. Well, Nancy's passport arrived in the mail. I got a nice official letter announcing my application had been rejected. It seems that the issue date on my official birth certificate was two years later than my birth date, as shown on the document.

"So what?" I asked the passport person on the phone. "It is my official government-issued birth certificate." "We cannot accept a birth certificate dated more than one year after the birth date," the passport person responded.

I explained I was adopted when I was about two years old, and my birth certificate was dated then. "Well, just request a copy of your original birth certificate," they said. "But this is my official state-issued birth certificate." I countered. "Well, just get the state to issue a letter explaining why the date is two years later than your birthday," the passport person replied.

I tried to get an official letter from the state, but the state explained that the adoption information was sealed, and they could not send a letter confirming or denying I had been adopted.

My follow-up call to the passport people went no better. "Listen," I said, "I was adopted at the age of two, given a new name and my official government-issued birth certificate, of which you have a copy." "We need the original," she replied. We had reached a stalemate.

Fortunately, I was issued a temporary passport for the upcoming vacation and that temporarily solved the problem.

A few months after the vacation, and yes, we had a wonderful time, I jumped back into problem-solving mode. First, I needed to get a real passport to take another vacation if we ever got a chance.

About two weeks into the mind-numbing and seemingly fruitless process of talking to countless friendly but unhelpful bureaucrats, I finally dialed the magic number.

"May I help you?" "Yes, I am having a problem getting a passport because my birth certificate was issued two years after my birth, because I was adopted, and the passport people said they can't accept one dated more than a year past the birth, and all the states people told me the certificate I have is legally my original birth certificate and the only one I'm going to get." I paused, waiting for the standard reply, "You need to speak to so-and-so in department 321. May I place you on hold while I go on break, during which time you will be disconnected?" But the lady at the magic number then asked for my full name, date of birth, and adoptive parents' names. I gave them to her. "Just a moment, please," she replied.

I could feel disappointment and frustration building inside me as I once again dutifully awaited the all-too-familiar deadline click followed by a dial tone sound. At least she asked a few questions before dumping my call, and by then, even that felt like I was making progress. And evidently, I was. She returned to the line and continued, but in a slower, more somber tone. "Mr. Cole, do you know anything about the circumstances of your birth and adoption?"

I was starting to get a little nervous and a little excited. I repeated the story I had always been told about my father dying in the war and my mother in a car accident and added that I never really believed that one. "I see," she said. I have your file here, and I can tell you what is in it if you would like." "That's great!" I exclaimed as my excitement level took off.

"Well, Mr. Cole, are you sitting down?" she asked. Now, unless you are talking to the executor of a rich uncle's will, that is the very last thing you want to hear before someone gives you some news.

It is amazing how quickly excitement can change to fear. My heart started pounding, and my mind started racing ahead. The information she was about to reveal had to be bad, very bad, I thought. But what could possibly be that bad?

"Oh no! My father was Adolf Hitler, and my mother is still alive but serving a life sentence for eating her other children! No, no, maybe it's even worse; maybe my father was…" "Mr. Cole! Mr. Cole!", "What? Oh, yes, I'm sitting down," I replied.

In a slow and more caring tone, the nice lady shared the information in my file. She explained that since my adoptive parents were deceased and my biological parents' identities and whereabouts were unknown, my records could be released.

She went over the records with me, then paused. She was waiting for my reaction, and I bet she had heard a lot of interesting ones over the years. She told me later that most people ended up crying or just hanging up when receiving this type of background information. She said my "That's so cool!" response was a refreshing and unexpected change.

I finally had some answers! I wasn't even looking for them; they just came to me. At that point, I knew the circumstances of my becoming a ward of the state and the details of my adoption. I also had the paperwork I needed to get a real passport.

Armed with the new information and dates provided by the nice lady at the magic phone number, Nancy and I searched the newspaper archives at the library and quickly found several articles about myself.

May of 1999 was just a few months away, and my son Michael was coming into town for our annual birthday get-together. I was turning 55, and Michael would be 27. Michael's birthday and mine are only two days apart, and since he lived out west, we used the two birthdays as a good excuse to get our small family together. I waited for that little family gathering to share what I had learned about my early history.

Never one to pass up an opportunity to mess with the kids, I sat them around the table and showed them a business-quality presentation folder, the type with a cutout on the front cover to highlight a title in the middle of the first inside page. It did look somewhat professional.

I told the kids I had decided to step away from my businesses and become an author. The kids are never really sure when I'm serious and when I'm kidding, so at that moment, I was only getting blank stares in return. "This folder contains a preview of my first book," I announced. Their silence and blank stares continued.

Of course, I had no intention of retiring and certainly no crazy idea about writing a book. That was just a setup for the news I wanted to share with them. Things sure have a curious way of working out sometimes.

The front cover of the folder revealed the title page:

The Story of Richard Parker
alias "Baby Boy"
A story of hard times and new beginnings in old Atlanta

The kids were attentive as I began reading. "It was an early Sunday morning in July of 1944. World War II was still raging, and times were tough everywhere. Richard Parker was lying on the bed in his hotel room, waiting, unsure what for. He was getting hungry. Soon the police would come through the door, and his life would change forever. Tomorrow he would be front-page news."

I paused the presentation at that point and asked what they thought so far. Elaine, Tony, and Michael, being polite and respectful people, replied with polite and respectful encouragement. As they nervously glanced at each other, their expressions were saying, "oh boy, lots of luck with that." I didn't drag the joke out longer since they already suspected I was, indeed, messing with them.

The rest of the folder contained newspaper articles and official documents detailing the real circumstances of my first few months of life. I laid out copies of the articles and adoption documents for the kids to look at, and everyone really enjoyed learning about my early history.

The real story began on Sunday, July 2nd of 1944. A young blond woman with an infant checked into the Robert Fulton Hotel in downtown Atlanta. A witness later told police the woman was nice-looking and appeared to be about 18 years old. She had used the name Mrs. Richard Parker of Salt Lake City to check-in. Later, when the staff came by to straighten the room, I was there; the young woman was not.

After a reasonable period of time, the hotel staff called the police. The police quickly concluded that since the only things left in the room were me and a bag containing diapers and baby formula, the young woman was probably not returning.

I was taken a few blocks away to Grady Memorial Hospital, where I was checked in as "Baby Boy," which was not very creative, but it was accurate. My first official name, Richard Parker, was given to me a few days later.

The hospital reports noted I seemed to be in reasonably good health other than being underweight. A doctor's estimate of my age when I was found was used to calculate an approximate date of birth. Progress was being made in my life. In town for just a few days, and I already had a new name and official birth date.

According to one of the newspaper articles, "Baby Boy" was a hit with the nurses and was very well cared for during his stay at the hospital. I was soon deemed healthy enough to be placed in foster care.

I was so happy I had learned how I came to be adopted, but I still wondered who my biological mother and father were and if either was still alive. I speculated about the likelihood of having brothers and sisters out there somewhere and maybe even living in the Atlanta area. Before learning about being found in a hotel, I had never searched for my birth parents, although I was always a little curious. I did wish to know, but I think there was a little concern for what I might find. After all, maybe my father really was Hitler, and my mother was a cannibal who ate her children. The old saying, "be careful what you wish for", did lurk in the back of my mind.

I still did not know where I was born, who my mother or father was, or my real birthday. But, over the years, I realized that while those are things people like me would really like to know, I would survive just fine if I never found out.

What Day is it?

B y the end of 1999, we had recorded our second year of exceptionally
strong sales at the stores. Having money in the bank at the end of a
year was weird. It just didn't seem right, but the accountant assured us
there was no mistake. The leftover profits would not have been a lot to a
wealthy person, but it was a lot to two people who had been on a money
diet for ten years. The urge to buy a nicer house or some new cars was
strong, but common sense and the discipline developed over the years of
getting by on nothing prevailed.

  We decided to invest in some property we could build a house on later
or sell if times got rough again. After a few months of looking, we purchased
a 13-acre tract of vacant land not too far north of our office. The seller was
motivated, and the price was right. We were happy with our decision and
knew that we could build a nice little house on a hill in the middle of those
woods when we were ready, just like so many people dream of doing.

The good years and interesting experiences were stacking up. In 2000, our industry's official trade publication, Birding Business Magazine, came out with its first full-size, full-color magazine. Its feature article was about the Bird Watcher Supply Company stores and me. That publication was certainly not Southern Living, Time, or People Magazine, but I was right on the front cover and that made me feel pretty darn good.

Another fun experience occurred that same year. But, again, it was one of those "right place at the right time" events.

Cole's, our birdseed business, needed some quality video of our seed products and wild birds at bird feeders to use in a little "infomercial" about our company. After checking the rental fees for a commercial-grade digital camera, we realized we would be better off buying one for the amount of time we would need it. It was a very nice state-of-the-art unit like news crews were using, and I needed to get in some practice time to learn how to operate it properly.

It was a nice day, and I had positioned myself on our front steps and focused the new video camera on the bird feeding area about ten feet away in our front yard. Start, stop, zoom in and out, switch recording modes, and keep the camera steady on my shoulder. I began filming the birds moving around under the feeder and slowly learned to drive that camera.

Filming while giving myself directions, I got some good shots with the new camera. "All right, get that cardinal in the shot and follow it along the ground as it feeds. Oh, good, there's a male towhee, zoom in, that's better, now try to, hey, that towhee doesn't look right."

It was a towhee, but the bird I was watching in the camera viewer looked slightly different from an Eastern Towhee. I caught my thoughts wandering off track, so I made a quick mental note to check the video later and focused on getting other good bird videos.

"Ok, Richard, keep your mind on what you are doing. Do not get distracted. Steady with the camera, follow the subject, now zoom back a little to show more background; I think I'm getting the hang of this." After my practice session, it was time to play the video shots on the TV and see how the new camera and cameraman in training worked out.

Nancy walked in as the video was playing, and the first thing she said was, "That's not an Eastern Towhee! Did you look at that bird?" "What? What's not what bird? Oh, I forgot all about seeing it." I paused, took my mind off the technical aspects of the video, and looked again at the towhee on the screen. Oops! It was a Spotted Towhee, a western species not found here. We called the sighting into the rare bird hotline. Well, no one can say that rare bird sighting wasn't well documented.

Over the next week that the bird stayed around, many birdwatchers came by to catch a glimpse of the Spotted Towhee. The bird was given a nice little article in the newspaper, and I got credit for another rare bird find, the first Spotted Towhee documented in Georgia. Sometimes you are good, and sometimes you are just plain lucky. That rare bird record was mostly luck.

In 2001, our favorite landlord made us another one of his offers that we just could not refuse. He had a great retail location about to become available and said it would be perfect for another Bird Watcher Supply store, and he was offering it to his favorite tenants first. That man was a really good salesman.

We were in an economic slowdown period, and that made the thought of adding another store more frightening than usual. But the location was great, and the deal was too good to pass up, so Bird Watcher number four was added to our little chain.

The very next year, we were approached by a local competitor who wanted to sell his small wild bird supplies store. Buying another business was a different game, so I had to seek good advice and dig into a lot of "How To" books to be sure I did it right. We really liked the location, and with a little remodeling, a new sign, and a load of fresh merchandise, we had store number five and another new learning experience.

Where does the time go? It seemed as though Nancy and I were bagging birdseed in our garage just a year or two before, and all of a sudden, it was 2003; we owned five retail stores and a growing bird seed packaging company. But it had not been just a year or two. It had been 15 years since we opened that first little store and even longer since we started bagging birdseed in our garage.

Soon after I turned 59 years old, I started getting a little spooked about hitting the big "6" "0". Every time the thought of turning 60 started haunting me, I would pause and think about where I was in life and if I was satisfied with what I had accomplished.

I felt like I did when taking a timed test back in school, and the "five minutes remaining" bell would ring. Had I been focused and productive or had the time slipped away, leaving too little time to finish the test? At that point in my life, the answer was "yes, but." Yes, I thought I had done pretty well, but I wasn't quite satisfied. I still wanted to accomplish more and do better with the time I had left. For my entire adult life, I had those feelings. The "60" thing just rekindled those old anxieties and insecurities.

Despite my anxieties, I actually felt everything was going well. The businesses were running smoothly. Nancy and I had settled into a nice, sustainable work pace, and most of our workdays were low-stress routines.

One Thursday in late June was a perfect example of our typical workday. Arrive at about 10:00 am, catch up on calls, work on product orders, discuss plans, and handle the crisis of the day, and there always seemed to be one. By 4:30 pm, the workday was winding down, and everyone except Nancy and I was getting ready to leave for the day. We still kept office hours like we did when we worked in the retail stores, arriving at about 10:00 am and working until around 7:00 pm. Those last hours at the office were quiet and usually void of the normal workday interruptions. It was a very productive time of day for both me and Nancy.

My goal for that afternoon was to catch up on the entry of sales figures into the spreadsheet I used to track store performance. It was a boring but necessary task, and despite a very unusual and very annoying headache, I got one more thing checked off my to-do list.

Since I did such a good job with the sales figures, I decided to do something I actually enjoyed. Repairing damaged merchandise was one of my favorite chores, and it was waiting for me out in the warehouse. I always liked working with my hands and fixing things. It was hard for me to understand how so many products got broken in the stores, but it kept me furnished with an endless supply of "fix it" busy work.

Just as I started repairing a broken hanger on a wooden bird feeder, I remembered we had some French fries left over from lunch. I usually threw any leftover fries or bread out onto the parking lot for the birds, but only after hours and if no visitors were coming the next morning.

I remembered the fries just in time to catch Elaine before she left. It was the birds' lucky day; Elaine told me no visitors were scheduled the next morning, so I gave the birds an afternoon snack before returning to my repair task.

For some reason, I wasn't driving as we approached our house. It looked like our house, but it wasn't quite the same. The front of the house looked familiar, but somehow it seemed reversed, like a mirror image.

Once inside, things didn't get better. I felt I had entered another dimension where everything was only similar to the world I had known before. It was so strange. I thought I had some type of visual dyslexia. Something was very, very wrong.

I had just put food out for the birds, and then I was at home. The house didn't look right, and I didn't understand why Nancy, Michael, and Elaine were all there. They were talking about a boot camp. Nancy was calling it a brain boot camp. It didn't make sense to me, but Nancy had enrolled me in something. I didn't understand why I was going to a boot camp? I was not capable of comprehending much of anything that was going on around me, and only small fragments of my daily life were being recorded in my memory.

It had been almost a month since I fed the birds at the office. I had been in intensive care at a local hospital since that afternoon. I had no memory of anything up to arriving home.

Nancy later told me I was not feeling well after putting the French fries outside, and I wanted to go home early. A short time later, she found me lying down on the floor in the office hallway. She said I was alert and conversant but nauseous. I complained of a really bad headache and just wanted to lie there for a while. She thought I had the flu, but I wasn't any better after a couple of hours, so she called 911 for help.

I had suffered a severe brain hemorrhage caused by an AVM. An arteriovenous malformation is a congenital vascular defect. A malformed jumble of arteries and veins which allows a high-pressure artery to bypass the connecting capillaries and discharge directly into veins designed only for the low-pressure return of blood to the heart. That afternoon a vessel in the AVM finally ruptured, and blood escaped into the brain cavity.

Hemorrhages in any part of the body are very serious, but they are particularly problematic in the brain and have a high mortality rate. This is because the blood escaping into the sealed brain cavity increases pressure on the brain tissue. As the pressure increases, brain cells begin dying, and any functions they control become compromised. Also, any part of the brain previously sustained by the leaking blood would also die.

But I was back home, and there was some really good news. I wasn't dead yet. The bleeding had probably stopped soon after it started. If I had not been in really good physical condition, without a trace of high blood pressure, the outcome would likely have been far worse.

Then there was the bad news. The part of the AVM that had ruptured could start bleeding again, and because it was deep inside the brain, any type of surgery was far too risky.

From the moment the bleeding started, nothing could have been done except wait and hope. So, the plan was to send me home and give my brain a few months to mend. Basically, the doctors needed to wait for all the internal swelling to subside and for the old blood and damaged cells to flush out. Then they could consider methods to address the problem. The unspoken hope was the bleeding would not restart before then. In the meantime, I was off to brain boot camp.

I don't remember much of my first week there, but my ability to retain memories improved a little every day. The brain boot camp was actually the highly rated Shepherd Center for Brain Injury Rehabilitation and Recovery in Atlanta. Thanks to my wife's persistence, I was enrolled within a week of leaving the hospital.

So, why did they send me off to the "brain boot camp"? According to the stories they tell me, I wasn't very functional, and I spent a lot of my time repeating two questions, "What time is it?" and "What day is it?" over and over. I had lost the ability to store short-term memories. That is why I had virtually no memories of anything since the hemorrhage occurred. It was also why I kept repeating myself. Without the ability to store memories, every few minutes was a clean slate with no idea of what had transpired a few moments before.

The lingering memory issues made it difficult to do simple, normal things like taking a shower. I would find myself in the shower with the water running and have no idea if I had washed or not. Had I just gotten in the shower, or had I already washed, maybe several times? I finally learned to check the washcloth. If it was dry, I had just gotten in the shower, and if it was wet, I probably had already used it. When the wet washcloth test failed, Nancy would let me know I had been in the shower long enough. It was apparent I wasn't capable of doing the most normal daily task. But that's why I went to the Shepherd Center.

In addition to creating severe memory issues, the hemorrhage had destroyed the area of my brain that processes and forms the right half of my visual field of each eye. That left me with a condition known as Homonymous Hemianopsia. It's ok; I can't say it either. With this condition, a person sees only one side, left in my case, of the normal visual field of each eye. Unlike losing vision in, or closing, one eye, the right half of the view from each eye is not there. The books say this condition makes finding things and reading very difficult. It didn't take long to figure that out for myself.

I also managed to pick up several of the common problems associated with traumatic brain injuries. For example, I had become extremely sensitive to unexpected loud noises and sudden flashes of lights. Both trigger a defensive muscle reflex and verbal response similar to the one you would have if a firecracker unexpectedly went off just behind you.

Bouts of anxiety and depression had also become a daily struggle. Fortunately, none of those symptoms were life-threatening, but they can be so very annoying.

Despite all the problems with my brain functions after the hemorrhage, I had no physical impairments, and that became very obvious the first week I was in the hospital.

I definitely had no real memories at all from the time of the hemorrhage until I returned home, but strangely, there was one dream I vividly recall. I was at a wedding in that dream, and my daughter was the bride. The photographer came to me and asked if I would bring everyone outside for a photo session.

I went downstairs to where the bride and her ladies were gathered and asked if they were ready for some pictures. They were, so I asked them to go out to the garden where the photographer was waiting. As they headed outside, I hurried back upstairs to grab my suit jacket then headed to the photo shoot.

That was it. A short piece of a dream. But they tell me there was much more to it than just that.

Now, in keeping with my pledge to tell the truth in this book, I have to acknowledge that I can only vouch for the few dream details I remember and not the story of my actions during the dream. That part is only hearsay from my family.

According to the story my family tells, and they seem to really enjoy telling it, I had been in intensive care for about four uneventful nights.

They had been taking turns staying with me day and night and decided it would be alright to leave me alone for a night.

In the middle of that night, when all was quiet on the ICU floor, my dysfunctional brain decided I was actually at my daughter's wedding. And, like in my short dream, I had to get ready for a photo shoot.

Apparently, in record time, I unstrapped the blood circulation leg massagers, yanked the IV line out of my arm, discarded the heart monitor, put my hospital gown on like a suit jacket, opened in the front, of course, and rushed out of my room.

Reacting to the alarms I set off by going unplugged, the nurses were just getting up to check on me when I arrived at their station. "Which way to the photoshoot?" I was quoted as asking the stunned nurses. I do suppose that was a strange question coming from a man with a bleeding arm and wearing nothing but a hospital gown on backward.

The nurses' question for my family was more of a technical one. "How did he get unwrapped, unplugged, and out of the room so fast?" The hospital insisted a family member stay with me every night after that.

It had been a little over a month since my "head exploded," not an actual medical term, but I often use it because it seems to fit the situation. I had been at the Shepherd Center for two weeks, and I was making good progress. My ability to retain short-term memories improved and the memory sequences I was retaining were becoming longer and more consistent.

The Shepherd Center program was very structured and organized, similar to high school classes. We all started off in a homeroom where a teacher would read some things from the day's newspaper and encourage light conversation among those who were capable. We were all given a notebook containing our daily notes, a floor plan of the building, and a schedule of our classes.

I didn't realize it then, but each patient's notebook was a color indicating how much help or monitoring they may need to navigate the hallways, find classes, and participate in those classes.

The classes and other aspects of my day were tailored to my individual needs. The staff spent a lot of time helping me overcome my vision loss. Every day someone would walk the hallways and place a variable number of sticky notes on the walls in random places, some high and some low. My task was to walk the halls and find as many as possible. I was learning to compensate for the missing vision field. At first, it was challenging and exhausting, but everything that required thinking was hard.

Another class was designed to ease me into doing normal daily tasks like paying bills. For that exercise, I was given three utility bills and three blank checks. I just needed to write the checks for those bills. What would normally have taken me about five minutes had become a real challenge. I had not forgotten how to pay a bill, but actually doing it was severely hampered by my inability to stay focused on the task and having to restart each step several times. I was given 30 minutes to complete the three checks, and I did it in only 28 minutes. I was very happy about my little success.

I can laugh about it now, but at the time, the realization of how limited my abilities were, became the trigger for many episodes of crying, sometimes from depression, sometimes from fear, and so often from sheer exhaustion. But each day, things became just a little easier.

Towards the end of my time at the Shepherd Center, I was going out of the building on supervised walks around the little business area. They were seeing how well I could handle everyday activities like crossing streets and finding items on a list at a nearby drugstore. They even had me make a list of ingredients for a hot meal, bring the ingredients to the center, and prepare my own lunch.

My last few weeks of "Brain Boot Camp" dropped to three days per week to allow two days for me to get reacquainted with the real world.

On my first brief visit to my office, I sat in my chair at my computer, and everything seemed so familiar and so comfortable. I was actually back at work, and that felt really good.

My hands were on my keyboard, and my fingers were ready to type, but nothing was happening. I wasn't sure what to do next. It should have been so simple, sit at my computer and do whatever I do when I'm sitting at the computer. I wanted to check the sales numbers or run a report, but I couldn't quite figure out how to do any of those things. The "good to be back" feeling evaporated.

That moment truly frightened me because I thought I was much better, but I was forced to recognize just how dysfunctional I really was. But, as I sat there staring at the screen, an old memory of a similar experience came to mind.

Many years earlier, when I returned to work after my auto-wreck, where I suffered a bad concussion, I could not make sense of my own computer program design notes and diagrams. But, within a week, things started to come back together, and soon I was back to normal.

That recollection really helped. I realized I had done this before, and my mental capabilities would improve. Of course, it would take much longer this time, but I would get better.

I need to take a pause here from all my carrying-on about how bad off I was and mention my wife, Nancy. In reality, the first month after my brain event was easy for me because I had no idea what was going on. Nancy, however, was confronted with the stark reality that I was incapable of caring for myself or relating to her on any meaningful level. She also faced the constant threat, the possibility, that I could die at any time or, even worse, never get any better. Those days must have been utterly terrifying for her. I occasionally wonder if I could have handled that situation as well as she did. I am so fortunate to have Nancy as my wife, partner and best friend.

It had been almost three months since I entered the hospital and a few weeks after completing the Shepherd Center's program and things were getting better. My short-term memory was much improved. The bad headaches were not as frequent, and a little of my vision field had returned. My condition was improving, and the whole family, myself included, felt the worst was over.

But remember the old saying about the 800-pound gorilla in the room? It is something so obvious, but no one dares to mention it. My gorilla was the AVM in my brain. It was still there and even more dangerous than before. While my brain was healing, nothing could be done about it, so I don't think we talked about it much. But every headache I had still frightened me more than I ever admitted.

Dead at My Desk

By mid-September, it was time to take care of the AVM. There were two procedures suitable for my specific problem, embolization and radiation.

Embolization, the preferred method, employs a small, steerable catheter inserted into the femoral artery in the leg. It is guided, with the aid of X-ray imaging, up through the body into the brain and follows the arterial branches that lead to the AVM.

Once in position, the catheter delivers a payload of small plastic particles designed to lodge inside the artery and block blood flow past that point. The artery and anything it was feeding dies. This is repeated for all arteries involved in the AVM.

This procedure was preferred because blood flowing into the AVM would be stopped immediately, preventing the chance of another hemorrhage.

Brain scans, however, did not detect a clear pathway to the AVM, so the doctors had to go with their second choice, Gamma Knife radiosurgery. That procedure projects a beam of radiation from many directions to converge at the targeted area. The radiation overdose in the target area damages the cells' ability to reproduce and the target area slowly dies.

The downside of that method is the very slow death rate in the targeted area. That procedure could take many months to be fully effective, but the doctors had no other choice.

The Gamma Knife radiation process has three parts. First, the area to receive the radiation is scanned and mapped. Next, the map coordinates are used to program the Gama Knife to aim the radiation beams at the target. Finally, radiation is applied.

To get started, my head was fitted with a large, rigid metal frame called the "iron halo." The halo was held in place by four large screws firmly anchored into my skull. Then the frame was clamped onto the radiation machine's table. That prevented my head from moving during the procedure.

At my request, I was only mildly sedated so I could observe the process on a monitor.

To map the location of the AVM, they needed to inject a special contrast dye into the arteries leading into the area where the AVM was located.

The doctor maneuvered the dye injection catheter from my leg up to my brain. When the catheter was approaching the area of the AVM, the doctor injected a little dye to better see the arteries he needed to follow to get closer.

The next phase would have been taking the images and programming the Gamma Knife. I said, "the next phase would have been" because it never happened. The three highly skilled doctors on my team, and several associates in the room, ceased their doctor chatter and the neurosurgeon injecting the dye exclaimed in a somewhat excited voice, "I can get to it." A buzz of excited chatter followed that announcement, and I went to sleep. I believe they upped the sedation rate so I would take a nap while they held a conference.

I was in another room, and the iron halo was off when I woke up. I was groggy, but it seemed someone was telling me the brain procedure had been canceled. "Cancelled? They had just screwed a large metal cage to my skull, clamped my head to a workbench, ran a hose into my leg and up to my brain, and then, decided to take off early? Did the golf course call with an available tee time if they could come right over?"

Knowing how cynical I am, that's probably what I was thinking, but when fully awake, I learned the real reason for stopping the procedure was great news.

While injecting the contrast die into my brain, they discovered an arterial path adequate to allow an embolization catheter to reach the AVM area. They canceled the Gamma Knife procedure and rescheduled me for an embolization, their first choice. They were all very excited.

The team was reassembled three weeks later, and I was back on their workbench. When I woke up after that procedure, the news was pretty good. They were able to block off about 95 percent of the malformation. The neurosurgeon told me they were afraid to try for more because the AVM wasn't the only thing being eliminated when the arteries were plugged. Any other brain areas being fed by those arteries were also destroyed.

Being a really down-to-earth type of doctor, he had a simple, straightforward way of explaining it. "Trying to kill any more of the AVM would cause too much collateral damage, and if any of the 5% that is left ever bleeds, it probably won't kill you". So, I was cured, sort of.

The "cure" itself did have some consequences. The part of my vision that had recovered over the months was gone again, and the bad headaches were back as the healing process began again. But all things considered, I was pretty happy with the outcome.

I came away from that experience with a lot of knowledge about the brain, how our vision works, and first-hand knowledge of how great modern medicine really is. I also gained a huge portion of empathy and respect for people living with conditions that could cause their deaths at any time, yet still, pursue life as normal as possible. And the same goes for those people struggling to recover as much of a normal life as possible after any type of brain injury.

The following year, 2004, was a year of recovery, retraining, and adjusting to my new "normal" life. It was slow and, at times, so very frustrating because I was mentally struggling to do so many things that had been easy before. But time was my friend, and with every passing month, I saw improvement in my mental abilities and a lessening of the anxiety, depression, and headaches that had been my constant companion. I was even getting used to the new way my vision worked, or more accurately, didn't work.

Being back at work really helped. I'm not sure I was very efficient at the tasks I performed, especially early on, but work gave me a structure and a routine that forced me to keep trying. And I was doing so much better by mid-year; it was time to celebrate.

That May, I turned 60 years old. The big "6" "0" that had haunted me a short year before was suddenly a cause for much joy and celebration. Isn't it amazing how certain events can change one's perspective on life? Before, I was so concerned about accomplishing all my self-imposed "success" goals before turning sixty, and about a year later, I was so thankful and satisfied that I had simply lived to be sixty. I finally learned to appreciate what I had a little more and worry less about what I didn't have or had not accomplished.

My new attitude led me to think about the property we had purchased about six years earlier. Maybe it was time to build our little house on the hill in the middle of that property, and enjoy some of the fruits of our hard work before it was too late.

Evidently, my brain was working much better because I was soon going full speed ahead on my "build our little dream house" project. I had thought about that project often over the years, so I had the general plans all worked out in my head. I knew where the house would sit on the property and the direction it would face. The only major things left to decide were the house style and the exact floor plan.

I even thought about getting a golf cart and having a cart path wind through the woods and hills, and maybe buying a small utility tractor to help with property maintenance and tilling a nice vegetable garden. For me, that was the measure of having achieved the American dream. It was what a younger me, and many of my friends, talked about in those "someday" talks we all have. I had the land, the plans, and the finances to have my "someday" dream come true.

I also had something else, a nagging little sense that something wasn't quite right. It had been a long time, but right in the middle of finalizing my dream house checklist, an old friend came calling. That spontaneous moment of stunning mental clarity simply laid out my "someday dream home" checklist and made me compare it to what would best suit my current lifestyle.

With that brief, insight-filled "moment" came the realization that I was working on a dream home from an old dream. I realized that a nicer version of where we were living would better suit our current needs and lifestyle.

Our dream house plans, the updated version, were underway. The new wish list included a nice middle-class subdivision with hilly streets that would be good for walking, a grocery store close by for convenience, definitely a lot more space inside than our tiny house, and a small but nice yard. And while we were dreaming, we thought it would be great if there were a stream in the backyard. And, if there was a stream in the back, we would not want any neighbors behind us to spoil the serenity. I knew we were getting awfully picky with our list, but that is why it's called a wish list.

Nowhere on our new list was a reclusive cottage on the hill in the woods of the 13 acres of land we had bought. So that left me with a big question. What should I do with the land?

At that point in time, two things were happening to help me with the land problem. First, property values in the area had been shooting upward for several years as developers started grabbing the available multi-acre properties to cash in on that period's housing boom. Second, a very large tract of land adjoining our property was about to become a big new subdivision.

The new subdivision took a few years to complete its planning and legal zoning work and start the building process. During that time, I came up with the idea of building my own subdivision on our property. I sketched out what I thought would work and had a professional draw up the plans for twelve nice lots.

As the large development progressed, I worked with them to merge my property into their new community. Again, it was a good deal for both parties. I paid them their per lot cost for their subdivision's amenities, such as the pool, clubhouse, and tennis courts, and my lots became part of their subdivision.

My adrenaline rush went into overdrive, and I started calling contractors for quotes to put in two streets, sewer lines, and utilities for the homes I would build. I also started talking with a few general contractors about managing the construction process.

I thought I might need help with the construction process for three reasons. First, and least important, I had never done anything like that before. Second, becoming a developer and building new homes could not be my full-time job since I had to devote some of my attention to five retail stores and a birdseed company. And the third reason, I also needed to find us a new house since that was our new plan.

I was really excited by the new challenges, confident I could pull it all off, and I was well underway when I started hearing an old familiar voice. It started with subtle little hints that becoming a real estate developer may not be the best idea I had ever come up with. I ignored the hints. But that calm and patient but authoritative voice reaffirmed its message every few days. "Just sell the land, sell the land and focus on a new home."

Deep down, I knew the voice was telling me the best thing to do. But, my euphoric excitement for the new challenge was overriding my usual prudent, cautious approach to things. Fortunately, after a week or two of ignoring the persistent little hints, I finally told Nancy she was right. It would be better to sell the land and not develop it myself. Nancy always seems to know when to let me run and when to pull back on my reins.

My short-lived career as a real estate developer had come to an end. We put the property up for sale, and since all the legal and engineering work was complete, the project was ready for someone to start building houses.

Although I didn't get to build and sell houses, I got to name the streets, and I still think that was somewhat neat.

Once we turned our attention back to our original objective, which was to find a new place to live, Nancy and I didn't have to look far for a place that was right for us. The large subdivision our property had merged with would soon develop its phase II section at the other end of the subdivision.

Once developed, one of its lots would be on a cul-de-sac, have a nice stream behind it, and back up to a large flood plain where no other houses could be built. We immediately signed up to buy that lot and started looking at the home models available to build there.

The time just crawled along, but the day finally came when the new home was ready to move in. We put the old place up for sale and started planning to move to the new place. We were hoping it wouldn't take too long to sell the old house because, as is often the case with these situations, you do not want to go for a long period with two house payments.

Well, not to worry, as they say, we had a full-price offer for the old place at the end of the next day, and the buyer wanted to know if we could be out of the house in a week. We countered with "out in two weeks," they said "sold," and we started planning a big moving sale for the following weekend. The sale was a big success, and that made moving day much easier.

About a month later, we had a buyer for the subdivision property. That land turned out to be an extremely good investment, and its sale brought us a substantial profit.

That kind of payday was cause to celebrate, so we booked one of those worldwide cruises and ordered his and her Lamborghini sports cars to use when we were in town.

Yes, I'm kidding about the world cruise and the sports cars. When you scrap and save so long building a business, you don't let the money go so easily. You just can't do it. So, after we made a sizable donation to the government for capital gains taxes, and that really did hurt, we paid off the new home loan and used the remainder to feed our anemic retirement accounts. Maybe not as exciting as world cruises and Lamborghinis, but much more responsible.

After all that excitement, we settled into our nice, debt-free, middle-class home and continued working just like the old, financially responsible people we had become.

I don't know if it was because we were having fun or the years move quicker when you're older, but seven more years flew by in a heartbeat. It was 2013, and I had just turned 69 years old. It seems people over 50 often turn their thoughts to retirement, and I did it myself occasionally, but it was never more than a passing thought for me.

I know part of the reason I didn't dwell on retiring was that I didn't have a job so much as an identity. I didn't feel like I was slaving away like an unappreciated little cog in a big corporate machine. What I was doing for a living and who I was, had become the same. I enjoyed what I was doing and could not imagine who I would be or what I would do if I retired. I became anxious every time I started thinking about retiring, so I kept pushing it out of my thoughts.

Fortunately, I had one of my infrequent but always helpful "moments" a few days after turning 69. As those moments of clarity had done in the past, it simply allowed me to visualize my probable future if I stayed on the life path I was currently on.

I visualized myself at the door of my office, looking inside. It was only dimly lit by the soft glow of my computer monitor, but I could see my desk, and I saw myself slumped forward and lying across my keyboard. My left arm was stretched across the desk toward the phone; my head turned to the left, and my right arm hung limp toward the floor. I was dead, at my desk, at work.

While I had no problem pushing thoughts of retirement out of my head, that visual image, that spontaneous moment of stunning mental clarity, was there to stay. It had made a very compelling argument. Keep the status quo, the familiar, safe, and comfortable, daily routine, and die at my desk, or sell the retail stores and go bravely into the land of retirement and new adventures.

When I brought up the subject of retiring with Nancy, she admitted she had been thinking about it for a while and was ready. I was still hesitant, but I realized it was time to move on if I didn't want to die at my desk.

I spent the next several months investigating ways to sell a business and learned many ways to proceed. However, it was more complicated than just selling the stores, pocketing some cash, and walking away. While we wanted to get as much return for our hard work and sacrifices as possible, there were other concerns. Our retail stores bought a lot of birdseed from our birdseed company. So naturally, we wanted to ensure the stores would stay in business and continue ordering our seed long after the sale.

The other major concern was for our employees. Quite a few of them had been with us for a very long time, and we didn't want them to lose their jobs if a new owner decided to bring in their own people or if they let the business fail.

Sometimes the winds blow in the right direction; the stars are in a favorable alignment, and things work out for everyone. We were very fortunate to have good, hard-working people working for us. One of those was Julia, a senior employee who had been a store manager and was the current retail operations manager. We also had Ruth, a trusted, long-term office manager who handled the hundreds of important little things that keep a company running. It didn't take a genius to realize that Nancy and I weren't really essential to the daily business operations.

We met with Julia and threw out the idea of her becoming the new owner of the stores. We would set a fair price and finance the sale with low interest and manageable monthly payments. After considering our offer for a few days, she told us she appreciated the opportunity and asked if she could partner with Karen, a store manager and another great long-term employee. We thought that was a smart move.

The rest of the year was spent making a smooth transition to the new owners. Julia and Karen started the new year as self-employed business owners; Nancy and I were officially unemployed.

Distant Secrets

All my concerns about retiring, like losing my sense of purpose or having nothing to do, didn't last more than two weeks after we walked away from our retail stores. The anxiety of making that change quickly morphed into a calming realization that I no longer had to go to work. That thought still brings a smile to my face today.

The ample free time that became available with retirement was quickly consumed by all sorts of things we wanted to do. There was more time for travel, learning, exercise, and countless projects around the house. Retirement also gave me time for large projects like writing this book.

I began gathering information and creating outlines in mid-2017, two and a half years after retiring. It soon became my favorite hobby with no deadline in mind, except for finishing it before I die. As I wrote my story, I found the whole process much more challenging than I thought it would be. That was partially because of my compromised vision and somewhat because I had never written a book before. I also found the process much more interesting and rewarding than I ever thought it would be.

By the time I was writing about getting a passport and learning I had been dropped off at a hotel, the old urge to know my biological parents came back stronger than ever. I even started wondering about where I came from and if I was related to someone in the Atlanta area. I had read many stories about situations like that.

I believe my writing about that event stirred up my curiosity again, and my rapidly advancing age added a sense of urgency to the quest. The rising popularity of home DNA testing was giving many people like me more hope of discovering their original family. I knew it was probably a now-or-never type of decision for me.

A catchy ad for a DNA testing service caught my attention, and with great anticipation, I purchased a test and sent my sample to their lab. I got my test results about three weeks later, but they failed to match me with any close relatives. The hope of finding answers faded quickly, and I set those thoughts aside.

My thoughts did not stay aside for long, and despite my prior disappointment, my curiosity would not be denied. I knew that each testing service maintained its own database, and trying another testing service would increase my chances of finding a close match. So, with renewed excitement and higher expectations, I purchased another company's test, submitted my sample, crossed my fingers, and waited for the results.

One of the problems with DNA testing services is the results can take three to six weeks to come back. Not only was that a very long time for an impatient person like myself to wait, but it was a pause that allowed my worst fears to creep back into my conscious thoughts.

What if I find close family members who are really terrible people? What if I located my mother or father and they wanted absolutely no further contact with me and proceeded to cuss me out for contacting them? What if I found parents or siblings, and each of them is absolutely thrilled to meet me because they really need to borrow some money. There are so many things that can go so very wrong when searching for your unknown biological family. I began to wonder if it was really a good idea to open that door.

That second test yielded absolutely nothing to worry about because, once again, the DNA test results showed no close relatives. The results did turn up over a thousand third, fourth and fifth cousins, but those are really distant relatives. It was another depressing disappointment. The only hope I had left was that someday a close relative would submit a sample to one of the two testing services I had used, and they would pop up on one of my two DNA matches lists.

A few weeks later, Nancy spotted our neighbor Cheryl out for a walk and recalled that Cheryl had posted a comment on the neighborhood's Facebook page about being a member of a genealogical society. As Cheryl passed our house, Nancy and I interrupted her walk, explained my lack of success using DNA testing, and asked if she had any ideas. Cheryl said I should contact a friend of hers who specialized in helping people like me find their birth parents.

Cheryl's friend, Gerri Berger, is a genetic genealogist. That is a relatively new term that describes someone who not only uses information gleaned from a myriad of public records and documents, but combines that information with the modern science of DNA testing to improve the chances of identifying previously unknown relatives.

Gerri herself got into the field when she searched for her own family. She was soon helping others with their searches and eventually turned her expertise and passion into a business.

I contacted Gerri, and she walked me through the process and explained what we could reasonably expect to find or not find, how much time it could take, and the cost for that time. She also wanted me to purchase a DNA test kit from the service she used because it had a larger database and would expose me to more potential DNA matches.

I ordered, yet another, DNA test, and Gerri started working with the DNA matches found by my other DNA tests. She was attempting to solve the relationships puzzle that connects me to all of those matches and help pinpoint my birth parents.

That process is far too tedious and complicated to easily explain, so I'll just say that Gerri is very good at genealogical detective work.

About four weeks later, Gerri was excited and very confident she had determined my mother's identity. The woman was deceased but had a daughter who was still living, and Gerri was trying to contact her.

Gerri was also getting closer to pinpointing my father. Me, I was just getting closer to an acute attack of impatience.

A few days later, and for the third time that day, I was checking to see if my latest DNA test results had been posted, and finally, there they were.

I quickly checked the DNA matches list and noticed a Pamela at the top of the list, but unlike the people at the top of the other DNA match lists, Pamela and I had 26% of our DNA in common. I did a quick check and saw our percent of matching DNA indicated Pamela could be my grandmother, granddaughter, aunt, niece, or half-sister.

The lady's age was not listed, but a small family tree was displayed, and it showed her father was Wayne Brooks, 1923 - 2001. That would put him at the right age to be my father and mean that Pamela was probably close to my age. She was most likely my half-sister.

The reality of what I was looking at hit me. My mind started racing in two directions. It was so exhilarating to finally locate a biological sister, but I was also fearful of the unknown consequences of that discovery. "What do I do now?" was just repeating in my head like a broken record. I finally calmed down a bit and called Gerri.

Gerri pulled up my Ancestry account, saw the DNA match, and agreed that Pamela Brooks was a sister and that her father would also be my father.

Gerri asked if I wanted to contact Pamela and then offered to make the first contact for me without waiting for my reply. Of course, I quickly agreed since Gerri had a lot of experience making sensitive calls like that one.

Gerri left a message for Pamela, but there was no reply. The next day, Gerri left another message, and again, no reply. Gerri said that was very common. She would leave a nice, professional message saying she represents a previously unknown close relative who wishes to make contact, and the person she called thinks, "Yeah, right." If Gerri had called me with that story, I wouldn't call back either. Actually, I would, but only because I would be so curious about what type of scam it was.

This contact would have been a little easier, but Pamela's Ancestry account was not active, so she could not see her DNA matches, which would have shown me. But Gerri is experienced and persistent and managed to track down Pamela's daughter and explain what this was about. The daughter called her mother and convinced her to return Gerri's call.

Gerri got back to me with good news; Pam, who lived way up in Iowa, was excited to hear about her newfound "big" brother and would love to talk with me.

The conversation started about as awkward as I imagined it would be. We both admitted we had no idea what to say. It was the type of conversation very few people ever have.

"Well, tell me what you've been up to for the last seventy-something years," one of us said. We both laughed, started talking, and within a few minutes, it felt like two old friends having a normal conversation. I was amazed that she was as excited about learning of me as I was about finding her. My fears of a worst-case scenario evaporated as the details of our lives were passed back and forth.

During our conversation, Pam told me our father divorced her mother, remarried, and had two other daughters, Nina and Cheryl, and a son, Michael.

I was quickly in contact with the other two sisters. Their brother Michael is not in close contact with his family, but perhaps I will also meet him someday. Pam, Cheryl, and Nina were born, raised, and still live in and around Davenport, Iowa, a long, long way from Atlanta, especially in 1944.

In just a few days, I learned who my father was and found three sisters, their spouses, children, and grandchildren. Just as quickly, I found myself unable to keep track of them. I had trouble remembering all the names, and once or twice I could not even recall my newly identified father's name. I realized it would take some time to adjust to all the new information.

We had identified my father and contacted his side of my family, but identifying my mother was much more difficult because there were no close DNA test matches to confirm the relationship. Gerri had to rely on her skills as a genealogist and put in a lot of research hours to narrow the choices down to just one, Mildred Benton. The search was made even more complicated because Mildred's father had been adopted, so her last name, Benton, did not match the family name that the remote relatives' DNA had indicated. But Gerri sorted through all the possibilities and was convinced that Mildred was my mother.

Mildred had passed away only four years earlier, at 89, but her daughter Suzanne lived in Davenport, Iowa. Suzanne had been raised an only child and very understandably was highly doubtful of Gerri's assertion about me being her mother's firstborn. And, if that were true, it would also mean her mother, our mother, had left her first baby in a downtown Atlanta hotel. I'm sure that is not something anyone would want to hear or believe.

It took some time, but Suzanne did agree to take a DNA test to prove, or disprove, Gerri's claim that she and I had the same mother. The DNA results confirmed Mildred was my mother and Suzanne was my sister.

Suzanne and her husband, Jim, began sharing information and photographs of my mother, and I started sending them things about me. The process of trying to create a relationship that had been missing for more than seventy years had begun.

The whirlwind of information and photographs exchanged between my new family members and me went on for several months, and I'm sure I was the big winner in that area. My new sisters only received information about my small family and me, while I was receiving things from all four of them.

The two most emotional moments I had during that discovery period occurred when I first saw photographs of my father and then of my mother. I was filled with a warm and deeply felt sense of peace and closure in both instances. My lifelong 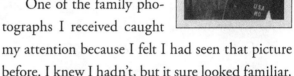 yearning to know who they were was satisfied, and yes, there were some tears, but they were the good kind.

One of the family photographs I received caught my attention because I felt I had seen that picture before. I knew I hadn't, but it sure looked familiar. It was a photo of Rollie Brooks, my grandfather on my father's side, and I did see some resemblance to myself in it. Then I remembered a photo of me taken a few years earlier. It was a fun moment when I put the two photographs side by side on my computer screen, Rollie's photo from the 1950s and my picture from 2012. The facial features, the

Richard and Rollie

hair, and the head tilt were eerily similar. Seeing relatives that I resembled was a new experience for me.

Seeing all the pictures and having conversations by phone and email was great, but I really wanted to meet my newfound family members. I could have gone right up there, but "up there" was Iowa; it was the middle of winter, and getting around up there in winter can be a little iffy. Everyone agreed that later in the year would be a better time for us.

It took a lot of schedule manipulations on everyone's part, but we managed to get together in Davenport in July 2019. Nancy and I spent a day with each sister separately, which allowed us time to get to know each other better. It was truly a wonderful experience meeting and talking with them, and I was sure there would be a lot of trips to Davenport in the future.

On the night before Nancy and I flew back home, Pam hosted a get-together dinner for everyone. After a nice meal, all of us gathered back around the dining table like a group of amateur detectives looking at facts, clues, motives, and timelines. All of us were pondering the mysteries of how I came to be and how the secret child of an Iowa teenager ended up in Atlanta, Georgia.

By the time we all met for dinner that night, many of my questions about my mother and father had been answered. I knew all the basics like birth dates, age at the time of death, family trees, occupations, and that their children thought highly of them.

I knew my father, Wayne Earl Brooks, who had passed away in 2001, grew up in Davenport, went to Central High School, and graduated in January 1942. Later that year, Wayne joined the U.S. Army Air Force and left home to fight in the war. He was injured soon after being deployed and was sent back to the states to receive treatment at a Denver hospital. At the end of June, he was given an honorable medical discharge and returned to Davenport. I was conceived a few months later, probably on Saturday, September 25, 1943.

Wayne had been married three times. He married Pam's mother in September 1946, and Pam was born in May 1948, four years after me. They divorced, and Wayne remarried in 1952. That marriage produced three more children, Nina, Cheryl, and Michael. Wayne married a third time, but there were no other children.

Wayne did many things during his career, including construction labor and working at an agricultural equipment and tractor company. At one point, he even co-owned a Suzuki motorcycle dealership in the Davenport area. Wayne also worked for and retired from the International Harvester Co.

I learned my mother, Mildred Jean Benton, also attended Central High School. She graduated on January 22, 1944, two years after Wayne.

She had become a well-known artist, and she also had been married three times.

Mildred was barely 18 when she married Ralph Bartholomew, whom she had known for a while. He was 24 years old and a second lieutenant in the U.S. Army Air Force. They were married in mid-February of 1944 in Boston, near where Ralph was stationed at the time.

That marriage was only a few weeks after Mildred's high school graduation and only four months before I was born, and yes, that does raise some very interesting questions.

We have no information on Mildred's or Ralph's whereabouts from the time they were married until 1947. Mildred noted in her photograph album that the war was over, Ralph was out of the Army, and they were back in Davenport. "When Ralph learned I was pregnant in 1947, he quit college and his job and re-enlisted as a sergeant. He was sent to Panama immediately. I had no desire for more travel, so I decided to become a single parent." It is unlikely we will ever know the real reasons behind their separation.

Their daughter Suzanne was born in early 1948, and Mildred's divorce from Ralph was final in June of 1949. Court documents showed Ralph was not present at the divorce proceeding.

In 1951, Mildred married George Sontag, a nationally known local celebrity, musician, and singer who made frequent appearances on radio and television. During her marriage to Sontag, Mildred devoted herself to her love of art.

In 1968, she married Joseph Dain, a director and senior vice president of John Deere & Company. By their own accounts, Joseph and Mildred were soul mates and remained together until Joseph Dain died in 1991.

I had learned a lot about my newfound family. I was also learning things about myself, like my government-issued May 20th birthday appears to be wrong. When I was found in the hotel, several people on the scene estimated I was about two weeks old. Based on photographs taken back then, that estimate was recently confirmed by an experienced pediatrician.

So, if I was two weeks old when found on July 2nd, that would make my actual date of birth about the 18th of June, and not the May, 20th date assigned to me later. It was nice to realize I am actually younger than I thought I was, if only by a month.

That was it. That's all we knew for certain. But, encouraged by the after-dinner wine, we started sharing our thoughts, speculations, and conspiracy theories about Wayne, Mildred, Ralph, and what really happened back in 1944.

As the lively chatter, encouraged by the wine, was bouncing around the table, Nina reached down and pulled a slim folder from a notebook, walked around the table, and handed it to Pam with a little smile and a "You need to read this." comment. Well, that sure got everyone's attention. The lively banter came to a sudden halt as we looked at Pam, looking at the folder.

Pam opened the folder, observed the papers inside for a moment, raised her head, leaned forward a bit, and looked down the table at Nina with a funny, inquisitive look on her face, then returned to her attentive reading.

"Well? Well? What is it?" An impatient chorus was building as Pam remained intensely focused on the papers in the folder. She finally put them down, looked up, and said, "Mildred and Wayne were married." "What?" we all shouted in unison. "Mildred and Wayne were married!" Pam repeated. "What?" and a few more colorful exclamations were repeated several more times before we got into the details of the new information.

Before the reunion, Nina had gone through her father's old things looking for personal items to share with me. She uncovered an official divorce document showing Wayne had sought and was granted, a divorce from Mildred, who "was not present at the proceeding."

The two were married on Sunday, December 05, 1943. Wayne had just turned 20. Mildred was only 17, still in high school, and a little over two months pregnant. The divorce was granted to Wayne on September 09, 1946. That was almost three years after they were married and just one week before Wayne married Pam's mother.

Learning that Wayne and Mildred were married forced me to go back and correct some previous notes to show that both Wayne and Mildred were married four times each, not three. I also added a note showing Mildred was married to both Wayne and Ralph from the time she married Ralph until Wayne was granted the divorce, about two and a half years later.

Nina's surprise revelation about Wayne and Mildred did answer one question. We now believe Wayne knew Mildred was pregnant, which is probably why the two kids got married. I suspect they were in panic mode and scrambling to figure out what to do going forward.

I returned home from our first reunion with a much better sense of who my parents were and who I am. But I also came back with so many questions still unanswered.

When trying to sort through my mother's and father's early exploits, I found all the dates, events, and names would just pile up into a confusing jumble of "who did what, when, where, and why," so I created a timeline list of events to help me keep it all straight.

When, Who, What, and Where

01-23-42   Wayne Brooks, my father, graduated from Central High in Davenport, Iowa.

12-11-42   Wayne entered the Army Air Force and was sent to Europe.

06-28-43   Wayne had been injured and sent back to a hospital in Denver for treatment. He received an honorable medical discharge and was returned to Davenport on this date.

09-23-43   I was probably conceived close to this date. My father was 19 years old, and my mother was 17 and a senior in high school.

12-05-43   Wayne and Mildred were married on this Sunday, apparently in secret. Mildred was a little over two months into her pregnancy.

01-22-44   Mildred graduated from Central High in Davenport.

02-16-44   Mildred married Ralph Bartholomew in Boston, three weeks after her high school graduation. She was five months pregnant and still married to Wayne.

06-18-44   I was probably born close to this date, four months after Mildred and Ralph were married in Boston.

07-02-44   "Baby Boy," aka Richard Parker, was found in the Robert Fulton Hotel in Atlanta, Georgia, 1,100 miles from Boston and 800 miles from Davenport, Iowa.

09-03-46   Wayne was granted a divorce from Mildred, who was "not present at the proceeding." I assume he applied for a marriage license and was denied because records showed he was still married to Mildred. A divorce from Mildred was granted to Wayne. At that point, Mildred was no longer married to both Wayne and Ralph.

09-09-46   Wayne married Janice Anderson 6 days after his divorce from Mildred.

04-11-48   Mildred and Ralph's daughter, Suzanne was born.

05-19-48   Wayne and Janice's daughter, Pamela was born.

06-29-49   Mildred was granted a divorce from Ralph Bartholomew.

Lingering Questions

Soon after I returned from our first reunion in Iowa, Gerri, my genealogist guru, attended a local Genealogical Society meeting. The guest
speaker was a writer from the Atlanta Journal-Constitution newspaper.
Gerri mentioned my story and its origins in the 1944 Atlanta newspaper.
That sparked interest with the newspaper to do a follow-up story. The article, "Baby, abandoned in Atlanta, finds his family 74 years later." appeared
in the Atlanta Journal-Constitution newspaper on Sunday, Oct. 02, 2019.
The multi-page article was a great add-on to the original 1944 articles.

The Quad-City Times newspaper serves the cluster of cities around
Davenport, Iowa and Moline, Illinois on both sides of the Mississippi
River. It also decided to cover the story since everyone involved, except

THE BIG STORY

SUNDAY, JANUARY 12, 2020 | qctimes.com | muscatinejournal.com | SECTION B

Search for parents leads Atlanta man to Davenport

Journey includes surprising discovery of artist mom

ALMA GAUL
agaul@qctimes.com

On Sunday, July 2, 1944, a slender, neatly dressed blonde woman checked into the Robert Fulton Hotel in downtown Atlanta, giving the name Mrs. Richard Parker, of Salt Lake City.

Later that day, a housekeeper entered the woman's room and found a several-weeks-old baby. The woman presumed to be the mother was gone.

Also left behind was a blue canvas bag containing a few clothes and a note with instructions on preparing the babe's formula and how often he should be fed.

Although World War II was raging in Europe, with the D-Day invasion of Normandy still fresh, the Atlanta Constitution newspaper ran a two-column photo of the baby boy on its front page, right next to the war news.

By then police had determined "Mrs. Parker" was a false name and had taken the baby to a hospital.

It was a sensational human interest story, with newspaper readers eagerly wondering who the parents were.

In time, so did the baby.

But it wasn't until 2019, about 75 years later, that the baby who grew up as Richard Cole learned through DNA testing

Richard Cole

that his mother was from Davenport, Iowa. She was born Mildred J. Benton but was widely known in the Quad-Cities as Ben Sunday, a prolific and respected area artist who died in 2005.

Most of her work was created in the 1950s through the early 2000s.

Contemporaries remember Sunday as a movie-star beautiful and strong-willed creator of hundreds of oil paintings, some representational, some abstract, and of ground-breaking collages using mixed media. Many are in private collections, including one owned by Deere & Co.

They also remember that she helped originate the precursor to today's Beaux Arts Fair, support the Figge Art Museum, and helped establish Studio 15, an art gallery. In 1991, she received the Harlequin Award for lifetime achievement in art from Riverssance.

Baby boy Cole's father was the handsome Wayne Earl Brooks, also of Davenport, who died in 2000.

Wayne Brooks

Documentation discovered this past summer revealed that Benton and Brooks married, apparently in secret, when Benton was still in high school. But they went separate ways after that, married other people, raised families.

As it turns out, Cole has four half sisters living in the Quad-City area, three who share Brooks as their father and one who shares Benton as her mother.

And as far as is known, neither Benton nor Brooks ever spoke about Baby Boy. It's possible Brooks didn't know of his existence.

How Benton, who was only 16 at the time, came to leave the child in a Georgia hotel just five months after graduating from Davenport High School in 1944 remains one of many unanswered questions in this story. The people who might have answered them are gone.

"We don't know what went on," Cole said. "There's some interesting mysteries left to solve."

But for Cole, finding the identities of his mother and father and meeting a sister he didn't know he had has been a joyous experience.

How Cole found his father

Some weeks after he was discovered in the hotel, Baby Boy was placed in foster care and eventually adopted. He grew up, made a life and raised a family, settling in Kennesaw, Ga., a northwest suburb of Atlanta.

FROM 1B: SEARCH, Page B3

Mildred Benton, in a photo accompanying her marriage announcement to George Sontag in the May 23, 1951, Democrat & Leader.

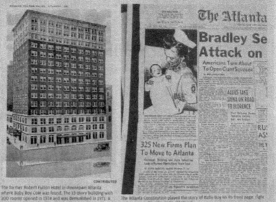

The former Robert Fulton Hotel in downtown Atlanta where Baby Boy Cole was found. The 15-story building with 300 rooms opened in 1924 and was demolished in 1971. A parking deck now stands on the site.

The Atlanta Constitution played the story of Baby Boy on its front page, right next to news of battles in World War II.

me, was from that area. The story, "Search for parents leads Atlanta man to Davenport," was published as a three-page special feature on Jan. 12, 2020. The collection of articles written by Alma Gall generated a great response from their readers.

In that Quad-City Times special, Wayne Brooks' three daughters spoke highly of him. Pam Williams said that "Wayne was charismatic and handsome and could command a room." Cheryl Hoffman remembered him as "firm." "He was a disciplinarian, but not in a bad way," she said. "We had responsibilities as kids. We knew what was expected. He was a hard worker and a good provider."

The article also quoted Nina McDevitt describing their father as "the world's greatest dad." "He instilled a confidence in us that we could do anything if we tried. And I think that may have been because he could do anything. He was always busy around the house, remodeling, adding on, and making things better. And he seemed to enjoy doing it. He worked hard at his job, and then he came home and worked some more."

It seems my father was a good man, a hard worker who always provided for his family and was respected by his children. To me, that says a lot about Wayne Earl Brooks.

The Quad-City Times focused more on my mother's career and achievements in society, and they were notable.

"Mildred Benton Dain was a widely known and respected artist who used the name Ben Sunday for her work because when she first began painting in the 1950s, 'A woman was always identified with her husband's name, and I didn't want to be identified by his name; I wanted to be identified as myself.'"

That's what Sunday told a reporter, in 1991, when she was being honored by Riverssance with the Harlequin Award for lifetime achievement in art. And when asked to name her best work, she replied, "I haven't done the best thing I ever did."

Sunday helped originate the precursor to today's Beaux-Arts Fairs that supported the Figge Art Museum during her career. It helped establish

Studio 15, an art gallery with several locations, and in the mid-1960s, Sunday opened and ran the Ben Sunday School of Art.

Son-in-law James Mann described her as "a feminist before being a feminist was popular. Certain women were trailblazers in art, and she was one of them. She could be very stubborn. She never let anyone tell her she could or couldn't do something. She never let anything stop her."

I was beginning to understand just how talented and well-known my mother was.

She was also the woman who "abandoned" her newborn baby. Which did draw a few comments back in the 1944 newspaper and again with the current articles. The 1944 paper's account mentioned the search for a "mother so heartless she could, and did, abandon her child."

While I understand those comments, I don't feel that way at all. I hold no anger or animosity toward my mother, and I don't feel I was abandoned, although technically, I was. I was simply passed along to others who could better care for me at that time. I also think about the intense pressures a pregnant 18-year-old girl must have faced in 1944, a far different time than today.

I recently saw some thirty-something guy on TV ranting about how his birth mother had ruined his life by giving him up for adoption. Really? He never knew her and was not raised by her; yet he thought she was terrible and ruined his life. As I watched him whine, I thought he should look a little more inward for the cause of all the problems in his life.

My mother did not ruin my life; she gave me life and left me in a safe place. When I first saw the 1944 articles, my thought was, "whoever you are or were, good job, thanks."

The two newspaper stories and all the details provided by my newfound family members have given me good insights into who my mother and father were and what they were really like. The more I learn, the more I realize how many of my traits, behaviors, abilities, and weaknesses are just like them. But unlike most people, I wasn't around my biological parents to acquire those things by learning from them. So, all of the many similarities I have with them are due solely to genetics. I find that fascinating.

My father has been described as athletic and a risk-taker, "the type of person who would jump from an upper story balcony into a motel's courtyard swimming pool, and did." He was a jack of all trades who could fix anything and a person who enjoyed fixing up things around the house.

A lot of that description fits me so well. When I was younger, my own need to engage in risk-taking behaviors was demonstrated by my years of cave exploring, working in the steel mill, and driving cars and motorcycles like there was no way I could ever be injured. I craved the rush I got by pushing the limits of what was safe.

My mother, Mildred, was an artist, and from what I have learned, she was a smart, strong-willed perfectionist who was driven to get ahead in life.

I excelled in my high school art classes and I even sold a few paintings. I later created and framed abstract art pieces and sold them in several downtown gift stores. I definitely had the instinct to create art, but I did not have the dedication it took to be great at it.

My mother had another pastime that really caught my attention. She loved wild birds, especially hummingbirds, which she incorporated into some of her art. In one of her photo albums, I found a picture of an artistically drawn list of "Resident and Visiting Birds" seen around her home. I could not believe it; my mother was a bird watcher.

In addition to art and bird watching, I share another love with my mother, raccoons. It is a little unusual, but I really like raccoons. They are intelligent, super interesting animals, and for over thirty years, I have put out a little food in the evenings for raccoons. I enjoy their company and their antics. Many of them became comfortable enough around me to sit on my lap or beside me and eat from my hand. As I learn to recognize individual raccoons, I give them names. I know  having wild raccoons around like pets is a little unusual, but I have really enjoyed my raccoon friends over the years.

I can't easily describe the feeling I had when I was viewing one of Mildred's photo albums and found a series of photographs showing her hand-feeding raccoons. They were her friends; she fed them, and she named them.

The whole "finding my family" event has been a humbling and enlightening experience. Now, no matter how much I still want to believe I am a very unique individual, I am forced to realize that I am, in so many ways, simply a fifty-fifty blend of my biological parents. But, after learning so much about them, I know I'm lucky to be sharing genes from Wayne and Mildred.

I had learned so much more about my origins than I ever thought I would, but my insatiable curiosity would not leave me alone. I still had too many questions that did not have answers.

Did Wayne and Mildred, who lived in the same neighborhood, have a long, short, or one-time romantic relationship?

Why did Mildred marry Ralph? There are pictures of her posing in his military jacket, so they did have some type of relationship for a year or two before they married.

Did Mildred's parents learn she was expecting and insisted she get married and she picked Ralph? Or, did Ralph just decide he wanted to marry her? And, did Ralph even know Mildred was pregnant when they married?

Did Wayne and Mildred meet in subsequent years and talk? If so, what did she say about her marriage to Ralph, and how did she explain why Wayne's child wasn't around?

What happened between the time Mildred and Wayne were married and Mildred married Ralph in Boston 73 days later?

Where were Mildred and Ralph from the time they married in Boston until I was found in the Atlanta hotel four months later?

And how did Mildred's two-week-old baby end up in an Atlanta hotel on Sunday, July 02, 1944?

It seems some announcer with a smooth, baritone voice should now ask us to tune in next time for the exciting conclusion of "Distant Secrets."

I knew there were many possibilities for how this really played out back then, but I had my own favorite theory.

From Mildred's photo albums, I know she and Ralph had some type of relationship for a year or more, but Ralph, being a soldier, was probably not in town often. Obviously, Mildred and my father had some type of relationship resulting in Mildred's pregnancy. Wayne and Mildred were secretly married in December of 1943, probably in preparation for the pregnancy becoming obvious.

In late December of 1943, I believe Ralph came home on leave and announced he would soon be transferred to a paratrooper training camp for a short period, then shipped overseas to join the war effort. I suspected Mildred and Ralph decided to get married before he left.

Just a few weeks after her high school graduation Mildred and her mother went to Boston, where she and Ralph were married. Soon after the wedding, I think Ralph and his new wife were transferred to the paratrooper training facility at Fort Benning, Georgia, only about 100 miles south of Atlanta.

It seemed likely Ralph was soon on his way to Europe, and Mildred had about three months of privacy in South Georgia to have her baby, and visit Atlanta, and no one would have ever known.

Is my theory pretty much what happened? We may never know. At this time, there is no other information to go on. Access to Ralph's military records may show where Ralph and Mildred were when I was born and if my theory is plausible or not. Unfortunately, the Covid-19 Pandemic has resulted in the virtual shutdown of all access to government documents, and access will probably be backed up for several more years.

I know the following story update will seem somewhat contrived, even though I said I would keep this book truthful, but I received Ralph's military records soon after finishing this book. I was still in the editing phase, so making a last-minute update was possible.

Getting those military records took a little over two years and assistance from a U. S. senator and a U. S. congressman, and a lot of persistence from their helpful staffs.

Ralph's records do show he was stationed in the Boston area when he married my mother and he was transferred to Fort Benning, Georgia before I was born. But that is about all I got right. It seems Ralph was in Georgia from March until after I was born. He was not shipped away.

I now know where Ralph was when I was born but I still do not know if Mildred was there with Ralph. I am still left with many possible ways those past events played out, but there are two, most probable, stories.

It is possible that Ralph knew Mildred was pregnant when they married and they decided it would be best if she would give up the other man's child. I doubt either of them was ready for a family at that time.

Mildred was a smart, resourceful person and it's also possible she devised a plan to be elsewhere for a few months while I was born. She just may have managed the pregnancy, birth and hotel drop off, with no one else knowing.

Confirming that Ralph was stationed in South Georgia when I was born seems to answer the question of how I ended up in Atlanta, and that was one more question checked off the list. I still don't know all the secrets of those people and those times and probably never will. But I do know a little mystery hanging over the story is not such a bad thing; it leaves something for my imagination to savor.

No matter what I learn going forward, I know a few things for sure. First, I'm so glad I learned where I came from and have had the opportunity to meet my biological relatives; they are all great people. And discovering my biological mother and father has given me a real sense of closure to my lifelong desire to know who I was and where I came from.

I also know how very fortunate I am to have been raised by Frank and Eloise Cole, my mom and dad. They gave me the love, discipline, and guidance I needed to find success in my life.

Now, as I'm finishing this book, for the second time, I am already wondering what my next free time project will be, and where it may lead me.

This is not THE END *because*

I'm still alive, and my adventures continue.

Credits

Emerson, Bo. "Baby Abandoned in Atlanta Finds His Family 74 Years Later." *The Atlanta Journal-Constitution*, 6 Oct. 2019,

Gaul, Alma. "The Big Story—Search for Parents Leads Atlanta Man to Davenport." *Quad City Times*, 12 Jan. 2020

Thanks to Georgia's U.S. Representative Barry Loudermilk and U.S. Senator Jon Ossoff and their staffs for helping obtain government records helpful to this book.

I must also give an extra-large share of credit and thanks to Nancy Makepeace, my wife, business partner and best friend. For over forty years she has given me her love, support and guidance.

CPSIA information can be obtained
at www.ICGtesting.com
Printed in the USA
BVHW070820130423
662287BV00001B/26